P.E.P
TALKS

(PATTYCAKE ENCOURAGING PARENTS)

Wyatt House books may be ordered through booksellers or by contacting:

WYATT HOUSE PUBLISHING
399 Lakeview Dr. W.
Mobile, Alabama 36695
www.wyattpublishing.com
editor@wyattpublishing.com

Because of the dynamic nature of the Internet, any web address or links contained in this book may have changed since publication and may no longer be valid.

Cover design by: Amy Stansell/in:ciite media
                    Kirsten Howard/Design House
Interior design by: Mark Wyatt/Wyatt House Publishing
                    Kirsten Howard/Design House
                    Deb Hash

ISBN 13: 978-0-9915798-7-7

Printed in the United States of America

P.E.P. TALKS

A **CAN DO** Guide
For Sharing **GOD'S BIG LOVE**
with **LITTLE LIVES**

JEAN THOMASON

Wyatt House Publishing
Mobile, Alabama

Miss Patty Cake is an amazing teacher/entertainer/worship leader for preschool children! This same talent for connecting with people comes through very clearly in her new book Miss Patty Cake's P.E.P. Talks. Her years of experience and fun experiences make a very entertaining read for anyone interested in preschool children. Every new parent who is interested in training up their children in the ways they should go should read this book.

Jean is a shining example of a woman who has followed God's call on her life and has done amazing things. Her influence will live on for many years to come through her songs, her DVDs, and now through the wise and funny words in her new book. Congratulations, Jean, on letting your light shine for Him!

Dr. Beth Watkins Cape
Director of Preschool Ministries
Whitesburg Baptist Church
Huntsville, AL

I know of no one with a greater understanding of how to reach the hearts of little ones than Jean. She embraces this as a high calling and the fruit she has to share will enrich your life.

Sheila Walsh
Author, *The Longing in Me*

It's about time! I have been after Jean Thomason to write a book for parents for years! For most of my life parents have looked to the church to teach their kids to be worshippers of the one true God. But the church can't do this alone. The church needs a partner and there is no better partner than whom God choose in the being to be the primary spiritual caregivers of their children, parents! (read Duet. 6:4-8) These P.E.P. talks will give you the skills to be the parents your kids need to be who God has created them to be. Great job Cake you nailed it. I love you and your sweet family and am so excited that the wisdom you have shared in conference and the truths you have walked out with your own dear children will now be available to parents everywhere. Don't just read this Mom & Dad do it!

Jim Wideman
NextGen & Children's Ministry Pioneer,
Author, Coach and Consultant
Jim Wideman Ministries, Inc
www.jimwideman.com

This book is dedicated to YOU,
THE READER, because you are
taking time to better equip yourself
as you speak into little lives.
You are obeying God.
THIS EFFORT MATTERS
FOR ETERNITY.

INTRODUCTION

"THIS IS THE DAY
THE LORD HAS MADE,
I WILL REJOICE
AND BE GLAD IN IT."
-Psalm 118:24

There — that is a verse I have known as long as I can remember (thanks, Mom)! I quote it, I sing it, I use it to correct my children, I speak it over negative or frustrating circumstances, and it is the quintessential **MISS PATTYCAKE** verse. And, when I say it, I mean it ... most of the time. So often I can forget the POWER of that verse — especially those two words, "I WILL." I WILL — meaning, I choose. It's a verb — something we DO. And that, for me, is the beginning of understanding PRAISE to God. Every day it is my choice to give thanks and praise to God.

5

But wait! What about my little children? How do I teach them to "rejoice and be glad?"

My preschool paraphrase:
"EVERY DAY IS A PATTYCAKE PRAISE DAY!"

Any of you who know **MISS PATTYCAKE** have heard me (her) say that paraphrased verse. If you watch the DVDs or listen to the CDs, I hope your children repeat it *ad absurdeum*! Because, "It is a GOOD THING to give thanks to God and to sing His PRAISE!" (Psalm 92:1)

The character we call **MISS PATTYCAKE** was originally called "PattyCake Praise" and was created to teach children to PRAISE GOD. The catalyst for this character was a song called, "PattyCake Praise" which was an effort to use the old "pat-a-cake" nursery rhyme, together with Psalm 47:1 which instructs us:

"Clap your hands, all you people!
Shout to God with the voice
of triumph and songs of joy!"

The "Patty Cake Praise" song, written by Nancy Gordon and Chris Springer, says:[1]

Pattycake, pattycake clap and play.
Pattycake, pattycake everyday.
Pattycake, pattycake praise the Lord.
Pattycake, pattycake praise!

Those lyrics, along with the words of Psalm 8:2, "Through the praise of children and infants you have established a stronghold against your enemies," fueled the idea to have this fun, colorful, musical, costumed friend/teacher, sort of Captain Kangaroo or Barney meets the Romper Room lady with a bit of Mr. Rogers wrapped up like *Playhouse Disney*, *Blue's Clues* or *Sesame Street*, and they all go to Sunday School. (And some of you have no idea who these characters are!) She would sing songs that teach Bible stories, praise, games and activities with a biblical worldview centering on the ONE GOD who made us and who loves us, and who sent Jesus, His one and only Son to live, die, and live again so we can be in His family forever!

WHEW! I know — big job, right? So look at this:

> **"Nursing infants are gurgling choruses about you; toddlers shout the songs that will drown out enemy talk and silence atheistic babble."**
>
> Psalm 8:2
> (*The Message*)

When I read that verse, it was as if I heard God say, "So, who is going to teach those songs to infants and toddlers?" Then I gave that answer ... that OPTIONAL ANSWER, the answer Isaiah gave when he saw the Lord, and heard the same question, "Who shall I send? And who will go for us? And Isaiah said, "Here I am. Send me!" (Isaiah 6:8).

You should be careful when you say, 'YES' to God, because He will take you seriously, and send you out, and you never know exactly where you will go or *what you will look like.* I have now, for more than 20 years, been dressed in a kelly green jumper with two hands and one heart appliqued on three pockets over a striped or polka dot blouse, tights, Mary Jane shoes over bobby socks, and a fun hat with a big bow or flower sticking out of it. Some may think this is foolish, but I remind myself, "God uses the foolish things of the world to confound the wise." (1 Corinthians 1:25) For these last 20 years, it has pleased God to use the "foolishness" of a costumed character to communicate His love and truth through music to hundreds of thousands of children! YAY GOD!!

PRAISE is a game changer. If you will practice praise by yourself, with your children, and do it often, it will change YOU. It will change the way you deal with your circumstances, and it will change the atmosphere in your home, and THAT will affect all your relationships! Because I have experienced the POWER OF PRAISE, and the change it makes, I have chosen the word "PRAISE" to be your guide in this HANDBOOK OF HELP. I, MISS PATTYCAKE, will be your tour guide (Ha! I just laughed when I typed that).

Let's begin!

READY! SET! GO!

P.E.P. TALKS
(Pattycake Encouraging Parents)

PRIVILEGED & PLACED TO PARENT

CAREFULLY CHOSEN

"Children are a gift from the Lord.
The fruit of the womb is a reward."

-Psalm 127:3

CONGRATULATIONS! YOU HAVE WON THE PRIZE! You get the reward! The incredible opportunity to love, protect, care for, and help shape a new life. WOW ... that's ... terrifying.

When we brought home our tiny first baby, I was giddy! My husband and I were enamored with that little blond girl with the loud voice. She was my dream come true. For me, pregnancy and delivery had been a lovely experience. I had never felt better in my life during those nine months and that epidural was the BOMB! I was made for birthin' babies! I had lots of help in those early weeks; my mom came, my mother-in-law, my sister, some friends, and they cooked and cleaned and held the baby, and I slept and nursed. It was all dreamy ... for awhile.

Then, they all left.

My husband went to work, and left me home — alone — with that tiny screaming, eating machine. If I hadn't had a phone I may not be here today! I called my mother every day, and my best friend, who had her baby four weeks earlier, and we talked each other off the cliffs. I devoured every page of the baby books I had, read my Bible, prayed OUT LOUD a lot, and slept little. In those days, I did *not* feel I had won a prize, I felt like I was running a marathon without training!

I had heard horror stories of what might happen, and believed them! The "what-ifs" threatened to keep me awake at night. Every little sound — or lack of sound — sent me rushing into her room. I listened to the voice in my head:

What was I thinking?
I can't do this!
I am going to be a terrible mother!
I am not sure
I even LIKE children!

I couldn't stop these thoughts.
Sound familiar?

Check this out:[2]

Research shows that 75-98% of mental, physical and behavioral illnesses come from our thought life. We are constantly reacting to circumstances and events, and as this cycle goes on, our brain's become shaped by the process in either a positive, good-quality-of-life direction or a negative, toxic, poor-quality-of-life. It is the quality of our thinking and choices and reactions that determine our brain architecture and resultant quality of the health of our spirit soul and body.

-Dr. Caroline Leaf

Why did I quote that right here in the first chapter? Because some of us are slaves to our negative and fearful thoughts regarding parenting or caregiving. When these lies and fears assaulted me, I prayed a one word prayer: "HELP!" I knew I had to change my *stinking thinking*. Without fail, the Holy Spirit, in His kindness and brilliance, would drop a truth into my head like:

"Whenever I am afraid I will trust in You."
Psalm 56:3 (thanks VBS)

. . . .

"I can do all things through Christ who strengthens me."
Philippians. 4:13

. . . .

"God has given us all things (everything we need) pertaining to life and godliness."
1 Peter 2:3

. . . .

"We take captive every thought to make it obedient to Christ."
2 Corinthians 10:50

The living Word of God is our best defense against the lies in our heads. Just remember where those lying thoughts originate … from the "father of lies." Also remind yourself when Jesus was tempted by that liar, the only words He spoke were, "It is written …" (Luke 4:4) Jesus knew God's word is "… alive and active and full of power." (Hebrews 4:12)

You and I have that same weapon against lies, fears, doubts, and other sordid condemnation. And we need it! I encourage you to arm yourself with these verses as you walk through your day and declare them. Say them out loud to any ears that may be listening. I wrote them on sticky notes and put them on my mirror and above my kitchen sink. I reminded myself, "God doesn't make mistakes and I was sovereignly, CAREFULLY CHOSEN to be this child's mother. Again, that one word prayer ... "HELP!"

Here is the thing ... God is waiting for *us* to ask for *His* help! Often I have heard this statement, "God is a gentleman." He does not force His way into our lives. He urges us, then waits for our invitation (or desperate cry). Jesus said, "Here I am! I stand at the door and knock. If anyone hears my voice and opens the door, I will come in ..." (Revelation 3:20)

"The Lord longs to be gracious to you, He waits on high to have compassion."
Isaiah 30:18

It's even better in this translation:

"So the LORD must wait for you to come to him so he can show you his love and compassion. For the LORD is a faithful God. Blessed are those who wait for his help."
(NLT)

After reading these scriptures, I hope you took a long relaxing breath. If not, just do that now. GO ON! There ... better? No matter where you are in this journey of caring for children, these words from God can give you REST AND PEACE. Say this out loud, "I am not alone. God is with me. He is my help. I can trust Him." Don't forget to thank God for the people who are on this journey with you. Their prayers and encouragement are further reminders of God's daily help.

In her book *Soul Retreat for Moms*, my friend, Melinda Mahan says:

> *Today the Lord is offering to take your hand and walk beside you on life's journey. He wants to be not only your companion, but your guide and protector as well. Although you may be hurt by an occasional stumble, you will not be destroyed by a headlong fall as long as you are walking hand in hand with Him.*[3]

Choose to take God's hand and join your heart with his. Just as a toddling child becomes more and more sure of his steps as he holds a parent's hand, so your steps will become firm as you walk with the Lord. He will meet all your needs, and you will experience the incredible reality that you are not alone."

GRADUATING

Will you indulge me as I share a bit more about my journey? When my children were one and two (16 months apart), I was looking for creative ways to talk to them about spiritual things — ways that were developmentally appropriate. I knew the clear command of God to parents from Deuteronomy 6:7, "Talk to your children about the Lord ..." I also knew a child responds much better to music than to spoken words.

Singing is a common occurrence in my house. As a worship leader, hymns and praise songs are sung around the house ... A LOT!

One day, I was encouraging 3-year old Marilyn to sing along with me, "*He is exalted, the King is exalted on high* ..." (Twila Paris) A bit confused, she looked up at me and asked, "Mommy, why is God so tired?" Something was lost in translation ... she though God was exhausted! That was the day I realized I needed new songs.

I found them! New songs and a big idea came from another mother, Nancy Gordon. It was her vision to create a costumed character who would sing Bible songs, praise songs, wiggly giggly songs, and songs that teach colors, numbers, abc's — sort of a *Sesame Street* goes to Sunday School. Nancy and I took a few already recorded songs she and others had written, wrote a little story about a treasure chest from God, had a green jumper made with two hands and one heart on the

pockets, and — VIOLA! MISS PATTYCAKE
was born. The very first time MISS PATTYCAKE
sang for mommies with their children was at the
MOPS (Mothers Of Preschoolers) group at Dau-
phin Way Baptist Church in Mobile, Alabama.

It was the children's pastor who said, "Jean, this is a really
big idea! There is a huge need for ministry to toddlers and
preschoolers." That was sobering and challenging! I thought,
Well then, I'll do it! So I made some calls, started traveling,
singing for little ones and parents in churches, schools, festivals, conferences (even a private birthday party in Paris,
France ~ thanks, Darla) … and I still am!

During my early years of parenting and MISS PATTYCAKE
"praising," I (Jean) had the fabulous privilege of singing on
the worship team for the *Women of Faith* conferences which
traveled to cities all over the country. It was AWESOME! I
loved every minute of it. For almost 10 years I took part in
this ministry, and during those years, the MISS PATTYCAKE
opportunities increased.

It was clear God had a BIG PLAN for MISS PATTYCAKE as
I got busier and busier with children's ministry. I knew it
was time for me to step down from adult worship to sing for
children. It felt that way, a stepping down from a big stage
in front of "big" people. I knew there were many women
who could take my place and sing on that stage, but very few
were singing to little children. I wasn't really happy about
this. I loved the women I worked with, I loved traveling and

singing, and, as we say in Nashville, it was a "great gig." Then came the day when my husband said, "Sweetie, I think you are done with *Women of Faith.*" He doesn't mess around!

I am not sure how you sense God's direction. It may be a Bible verse that seems to keep popping up, a heaviness or sense of unease, a nagging thought, advice from more than one trusted friend, or an "AHA" moment. My conversation with God went this way,

> Alright, I get it Lord, I know how serious you are about children, and I do love this 'kid gig'. So I thank you for where you are taking Miss PattyCake, and I will step down to sing for the children.

Well, ya know, I have never heard an audible voice, but this one was pretty loud in my head as these words plopped into my mind,

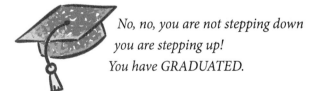

No, no, you are not stepping down you are stepping up! You have GRADUATED.

Graduated? Really? I had never, ever thought of it like that! It suddenly made sense. I remembered what the Bible teaches, God's Kingdom is upside down! God's ways are not our ways. In fact, they are often just the opposite. Jesus talked about this a lot! He said, "If you want to save your life, lose it," "don't repay evil for evil," "little is much, less is more, the first will be the last, and the least are greatest." And, who did Jesus say were the greatest? That's right —

LITTLE CHILDREN!

Mark 10:13-16   Matthew 19:13-15

Luke 18:15-17   Matthew 10:25

Mark 10:43   Mark 9:35

Matthew 20:26

GOD'S KINGDOM IS UPSIDE DOWN

"In the upside-down kingdom of heaven, down is up and up is down, and those who want to ascend higher must descend lower. And so anyone who becomes as humbles as this little child is the greatest in the Kingdom of Heaven."

Matthew 18:4

The Message)

I love the way F.B. Meyer speaks of this: [4]

I used to think that God's gifts were on shelves one above the other, and that the taller we grew in Christian character the easier we should reach them. I find now that God's gifts are on shelves one beneath the other, and that it is not a question of growing taller but of stooping lower, and that we have to go down, always down, to get His best gifts.

Our Father has given us (parents/teachers/caregivers) the ENORMOUS privilege and responsibility to teach and train these little ones. And, He has provided us with all the resources we need: His Word, the Holy Spirit Who is with us, and the wise counsel of the trusted family of God. As you work this field, planting seeds in little lives, TAKE HEART! This IS the high calling of God. It IS His gift. It IS an upgrade. The process of parenting will take you to a new place in your own relationship with Him. You HAVE been Privileged and Placed to Parent.

ENJOY YOUR REWARD!
(Don't be surprised when you realize you are actually having fun!)

RARE WINDOW
OF OPPORTUNITY

These first few years of a child's life are a sacred space. They form the foundation for life. Those of us who care for children during this time have the rare opportunity to participate in this formation. At this stage, little children have the greatest capacity for learning. Our job, in addition to keeping them alive and well, is helping them learn the BIG story of the Bible so they will have a strong foundation of God's truth which will help them live for Him.

These little ones are not only precious to us, but also to God. So much so, that Jesus said of them in Matthew 18:10, "Beware that you don't look down on any of these little ones. For I tell you that in heaven their angels are always in the presence of my heavenly Father." Jesus sternly rebuked his followers for keeping the children away from Him. He said, "Let the little children come to me, and do not hinder them, for the kingdom of heaven belongs to such as these." (Matthew 19:14)

We see how loved these little ones are. We know we are responsible, God helping us, for their spiritual formation, so how can we prepare for the task at hand?

UNDERSTAND THE TIMES

If you've read much of the Old Testament, you may be aware of the 12 tribes of Israel. These were the sons of Jacob who multiplied to become the Hebrew nation.

Before Moses died, he spoke a prophetic blessing over each of the tribes. These blessings were God's gifts, equipping His people for the good of the nation. (See Deuteronomy 33) Issachar is the name of one of the tribe and had the unique ability to understand what was happening in the world. Here is an example of their spiritual insight:

> " ... from Issachar, men who understood the times and knew what Israel should do ... That is, intelligent men, who understood the signs of the times, well versed in political affairs, and knew what was proper to be done in all the exigencies of human life."
>
> I Chronicles 12:32

The writer of Chronicles makes a unique observation of the men of Issachar — they understood the times and knew what Israel should do. What an amazing skill! The world is constantly changing. Are we holding on to the 'old ways of doing things' or are we taking the time to understand the ways that our communities are changing? This is the challenge of the church in the 21st Century — to not only understand the times, but also to know what to do.[6]

-Dave Whitehead, Senior Pastor,
GraceNYC.org

You may think this is an odd scripture reference, but I was captured by a sense of urgency when I discovered it. So much so, I bought a necklace with a pocketwatch

hanging on a long chain, and I wear it often just to remind myself to "understand the times." Being aware of the culture, knowing what these children are facing in their future is paramount for us as leaders/teachers/parents as we work to teach them about God and His "great big world."

God speaks of this same urgency in 1 Peter 5:8: "Be well balanced (temperate, sober of mind), be vigilant and cautious at all times; for that enemy of yours, the devil, roams around like a lion roaring [in fierce hunger], seeking someone to seize upon and devour." And again in Psalm 90:12, "Teach us to number our days, that we may gain a heart of wisdom."

REALITY CHECK

"Whoever wants the next generation
the MOST will get them."

-Motivation Statement / Sherwood Baptist Church, Albany, GA

I was moved to see the above statement in huge letters across the wall at Sherwood Baptist in Albany, GA. I thought, *YES! Here is a group of people who GET IT!* This statement happens to be one of the core values of that church. Any of you who have worked long with little children, or have studied much about early childhood education and development will understand why this is so very important. We have a few, very short years to help shape the little lives in our care.

Ask yourself this question, 'Who, in our culture, wants the next generation?' I would say there are many answers. Think of all that competes for the attention of children: art, education, sports, dance, movies, internet, etc. These are not all "bad," but most are "God-less." Even if we make the excellent effort of getting our children to church on a regular basis, the hours spent there add up to maybe 50 in a year. But moms and dads get between 2,000 to 3,0000 flexible hours in the home every year. As parents/caregivers, you and I have all the time we need to talk to our children about God.

> If we don't teach our children who God IS, someone else will teach them everything that HE ISN'T.[7]
> Darlene Schacht
> [emphasis mine]

George Barna, author and Christian pollster, after two years of researching child development and children's ministry said this:

> "When it comes to grasping the substance, the subtleties and the implications of the Christian faith, don't adults possess the greatest learning and intellectual capacities? Strategically, isn't it more important for us to equip adults so that they can use their gifts and resources to advance the Kingdom? No, no, no and

no. In retrospect, my view was so far off the mark that not only have I missed the boat — I missed the entire ocean! Ministry to children is the single most important work in the Kingdom of God." And even more to the point, "The most significant aspect of every person's life is his or her spiritual health ... Every dimension of a person's experience hinges on his or her moral and spiritual condition." [8]

- Transforming Children Into Spiritual Champions

Here are the findings of the Barna Institute: (and these are from 2004):

- 85% of all born again believers came to salvation by 8 years of age.
- By the age of 9, most of the moral and spiritual foundations of a child are in place.
- A child's character is almost fully formed by age 6.[9]

I was stunned when I first read these statistics. By the time I knew these to be true, I had been working with churches as **MISS PATTYCAKE** for years, and occasionally bumping into this ideology which was often, "Oh, just give them some crayons and paper, sing some little songs, feed them some crackers, and when they get older and can understand, <u>then</u> we will share the gospel."

WHAT!!?? No, no, no, noooo — do not wait! Do it NOW. Talk, sing, read to your children about God, even before you think they can understand the words. (We'll delve into this more in Chapter 4.)

"BRAINWASHING"

One day I was singing as **MISS PATTYCAKE** and telling the audience of children and parents about GOD. **MISS PATTYCAKE** always says, "God made me! God loves me! YAY GOD!" After the concert, a woman stopped me and asked, "Don't you feel you are brainwashing these children?" *Hmmmmm*, I thought a few seconds and said, "YES! That's our JOB." And not just any brainwashing, but washing with the water of the Word of God. (Ephesians 5:26) We can sing, read and teach our little ones from the Bible, trusting God will use His living word to work where we can't see. It is undergound activity. My friend, Ginnie Johnson, calls it "secret gardening."

● ● ● ● ● ● ● ● ● ● ● ● ● ● ● ● ● ●

The earliest messages that the brain receives have an enormous impact. Imprinting takes place EARLY. Early brain development is the foundation of human adaptability and resilience, but these qualities come at a price. Because experiences have such a great potential to affect brain development, children are especially vulnerable to persistent negative influences during this period. On the other hand, these early years are a window of opportunity for parents, caregivers, and communities: positive early experiences have a huge effect on children's chances for achievement, success, and happiness.[10]

-urbanchildinstitute.org

● ● ● ● ● ● ● ● ● ● ● ● ● ● ● ● ● ● ●

The first three years of life are a period of incredible growth in all areas of a baby's development. A newborn's brain is about 25 percent of its approximate adult weight. But by age 3, it has grown dramatically by producing billions of cells and hundreds of trillions of connections, or synapses, between these cells. While we know that the development of a young child's brain takes years to complete, we also know there are many things parents and caregivers can do to help children get off to a good start and establish healthy patterns for life-long learning.[11]

-National Center for Infants, Toddlers and Families

● ● ● ● ● ● ● ● ● ● ● ● ● ● ● ● ● ● ●

For a number of reasons, the two years leading to the fifth birthday are a unique and critical period during which you can shape the entire gamut of your child's attitudes and understanding. Developments in his intellect and speech will enable you to communicate with him in much more sophisticated ways. He will still be intensely curious about the world around him and is now better equipped to learn about it. More important, he will also want to understand how you see things both great and small and what is important to you. Whether the topic is animals, trucks, the color of the sky, or the attributes of God, he will be all ears (even though his mouth may seem to be in perpetual motion) and deeply concerned about what you think.

This wide-eyed openness will not last forever. While you will greatly influence his thinking throughout childhood, during the coming months you will have an important window of opportunity to lay foundations that will affect the rest of his life. No one can do this job perfectly; therefore generous doses of humility and much time in prayer are definitely in order for this phase of parenting.[12]

-Adapted from <u>Complete Guide to Baby</u>
<u>& Child Care</u>

● ● ● ● ● ● ● ● ● ● ● ● ● ● ● ● ● ● ●

George Barna states:[13]

The research is very clear: if Jesus is not already part of their lives by the time they leave junior high school, the chances of them accepting Him as their Lord and savior is very slim (6%, to be exact). With children, it is just the opposite. The greatest evangelical window currently available is among young children.

● ● ● ● ● ● ● ● ● ● ● ● ● ● ● ● ● ● ●

R. S. Lee, the author of *Your Growing Children and Religion*, says it this way:[14]

> *The first seven years [of life] constitute the period for laying the foundations of religion. This is the most important period in the whole of a person's life in determining his later religious attitudes.*

Give me a child until he is 7, and I will show you the man.[15]
St. Ignatius of Loyola
Founder, Society of Jesuits

Research has clearly substantiated the Bible verse, "Train up a child in the way he should go, and when he is old he will not depart from it." (Proverbs 22:6) So ... go ahead ... do what's best for your child(ren) by BRAINWASHING!

JELL-O®

One day when my children were little, I took them on a "field trip" to the mall. HA! Anything to get them out of the house and ME out of the mess! Does that sound familiar? Well, on this day I saw something I will never forget. You know how there are signs and ads on big posters and on kiosks along the mall? One of these caught my attention because of the color (big surprise). It pictured a tiered Jell-O® mold, bright green, with a large goldfish in the middle of the Jell-O®. The caption said:

A CHILD'S MIND IS LIKE JELLO, THE IDEA IS TO PUT THE GOOD THINGS IN BEFORE IT SETS!

That was awesome! I've never forgotten that picture. So, let's talk about how a child's mind 'sets':

- 95% of all synapses in our brains connect by age 2
- The foundation of character of every person is set by age 2
- The personality is almost completely in place by age 6[16]

-George Barna
Transforming Children Into Spiritual Champions

YIKES! What a REALITY CHECK! "Dear God! Help me know which good things to put in before it sets! Amen!"

My sister is an elementary school teacher. For the last 30 years she has worked tirelessly and sacrificially with young children. She is the best example I know of someone who takes advantage of the "window of opportunity." She has one school year to impact, for eternity, the lives in her care. She is underpaid, often under appreciated, and overworked. She doesn't care. She knows "her labor is not in vain." A few years ago I cross stitched these words for her, to help "spur her on to love and good deeds." (Hebrews 10:24):[17]

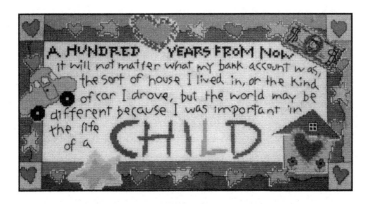

A HUNDRED YEARS FROM NOW it will not matter what my bank account was, the sort of house I lived in, or the kind of car I drove, but the world may be different because I was important in the life of a CHILD

Dave Stone, in his book, *Raising Your Kids to Love the Lord*, says:[18]

Let's face it. Only perfect parents raise perfect children. (Last time I checked, there were no perfect children and no perfect parents either!) There is no foolproof plan. And there's this little detail called free will, which will determine the spiritual commitment level of your children when they are grown. On the other hand, Christian homes don't just happen; neither do kids who love the Lord. There is a lot we can do to help determine the outcome of our children's spiritual lives. We can become intentional in our efforts. We can pave the way for them. We can model true faith and continually pray that God will transform their hearts. ... The earlier you begin the process, the better — but it's never too late.

GET SAD, NOT MAD

You know those days when things just happen? Frustrating things, messy things, broken things, disobedience, things that just make you mad? Right? Like every hour? My knee jerk reac-   tion is anger. Not huge anger, but it isn't pretty. And, I am a naturally LOUD woman, so my outside voice can hurt your ears ... and your feelings. I do not like this about myself, especially around children. I prayed often about it when my children were toddlers, then preschoolers. I cannot remember who suggested this to me ... when I discovered this "key." What "key," you ask? The key that helped lock the door on my loud, ugly anger was to "Get sad, not mad." Something clicked for me and I went into actress mode! If a drink spilled at the table, I would say, "Awww, poor milk. It wanted to be in your tummy, but now it's all over the table and the floor. Poor milk. Let's clean it up." My kids loved it. They would take a paper towel and wipe the milk and say, "Sorry milk," and other silly things.

TEACHING TO FOLLOW = DISCIPLINE

DISCIPLINE:
Training expected to produce a specific
character or pattern of behavior,
especially training that produces moral
or mental improvement.[19]
-Websters Dictionary

The idea of "sad not mad" works in disciplining. When children disobey, and they WILL, you can say, "I'm so sorry you didn't obey. Now I have to discipline you. Next time will you please obey so we can be happy and not sad?" Of course I heard this objection, "NO Mommy, you don't have to if you don't want to." God would help me remember that my highest obedience is to Him, and the Word of God says if we love our children, we will discipline them.

• • • • • • • • • • • • • • • • • • •

"Whoever spares the rod hates his son, but he who loves him is diligent to discipline him."
Proverbs 13:24

• • • • • • • • • • • • • • • • • • •

"For the moment all discipline seems painful rather than pleasant, but later it yields the peaceful fruit of righteousness to those who have been trained by it."
Hebrews 12:11

• • • • • • • • • • • • • • • • • • •

"Do not withhold discipline from a child;
if you strike him
with a rod, he will not die.
If you strike him with the rod,
you will save his soul from Sheol. My son, if your
heart is wise, my heart too will be glad."
Proverbs 23:13-15

● ● ● ● ● ● ● ● ● ● ● ● ● ● ● ● ● ● ●

"Train up a child in the way he should go;
even when he is old he will not depart from it."
Proverbs 22:6

● ● ● ● ● ● ● ● ● ● ● ● ● ● ● ● ● ● ●

"Folly is bound up in the heart of a child,
but the rod of discipline drives it far from him."
Proverbs 22:15

● ● ● ● ● ● ● ● ● ● ● ● ● ● ● ● ● ● ●

"Fathers, do not provoke your children to anger,
but bring them up in the discipline
and instruction of the Lord."
Ephesians 6:4

● ● ● ● ● ● ● ● ● ● ● ● ● ● ● ● ● ● ●

"Discipline your son, and he will give you rest;
he will give delight to your heart."
Proverbs 29:17

● ● ● ● ● ● ● ● ● ● ● ● ● ● ● ● ● ● ●

If you've ever known kids who are not regularly disciplined by their parents, you've probably seen some very stark examples of why it's important to discipline children. Discipline is not only good for children, it is necessary for their happiness and well-being. Discipline is as vital for healthy child development as nutritious food, physical and cognitive exercises, love, and other basic needs. Without discipline, children lack the tools necessary to navigate relationships and challenges in life such as self-discipline, respect for others, and the ability to cooperate with peers.[20]

– Katherine Lee, Child Expert

GIGGLE BREAK

WHEN (not if) one of my children required discipline, I would send the disobedient party to his/her bedroom and give myself a chance to breathe, pray, and let them think about whatever they had done. Then I walked slowly upstairs with the dreaded wooden spoon. One such day I sent my daughter to her room and when I arrived a few minutes later she had done something unexpected. Out of her drawer she had pulled every pair of panties and put them ALL ON to pad her little bottom. It was HILARIOUS! Pretty creative if you ask me. I so wish I had taken a picture. She giggled, and I laughed too hard to carry out the punishment. She said "sorry," I forgave, and we had a "grace" moment. I love that kid!

For me, most of the process of discipline was HARD. There was complaining, fussing, fighting, crying, and it was oh, so frustrating. I hated it! For crying out loud, I'm MISS PATTYCAKE and our life is supposed to be happy and fun all the time! NOT! I got tired of constantly hearing "WHY?" I remember thinking, *Please listen to me! I can see what you cannot. I love you and want to keep you safe. Do you believe me? Do you know I love you? Do you trust me? If I see danger that you can't see, won't I tell you?*

Wait … that sounds familiar. I complain to God in the same way. I ask "why," and fuss and hope God will change my circumstances! Being in this situation with my own child made me very aware of the parental care of Father God. He is MY parent and I know He loves ME. Will I trust Him like I ask my children to trust me?

Helen Young speaks of our RARE OPPORTUNITY in this poignant way: [21]

There will be a time
When there will be no slamming of doors
No toys on the stairs, no childhood quarrels,
No fingerprints on the wallpaper.
Then may I look back with joy and not regret.
God give me wisdom to see
That today is my day with my children.
That there is no unimportant
moment in their lives.
May I know that no other career
is so precious,
No other work so rewarding,
No other task so urgent.
May I not defer it nor neglect it,
But by the Spirit accept it gladly, joyously,
And by Thy grace realize
That the time is short and my time is now,
For children won't wait.

ALL ACCESS PASS

"God's divine power has granted to us all things
that pertain to life and godliness, ... "
-2 Peter 1:3 (NKJV)

Did you notice the word ALL? I am pretty sure it means ...
ALL, EVERYTHING, WHATEVER. I like to think of this
verse as the "ALL ACCESS PASS" to God's provision.

Have you ever had an "all access pass?" I remember the first time I went on tour with the *Women of Faith* conferences, and they gave me a laminated badge on a lanyard to hang around my neck. I didn't think much about it until we took a break and went out to lunch. I had to run back to my room for something and was separated from the group, so I came back to the arena alone. All the doors were locked since we were hours from the show, but I finally found a door with a guard. I knocked and he said, "Sorry, this is a restricted area. You can't come in." But I held up my pass and he opened the door and said with a smile, "Welcome." There was POWER in that PASS.

And we have God's power in His "all access pass." By the way, the password is: "Jesus." (But then you already knew that).

WHAT'S MY NAME?

My favorite time of a MISS PATTYCAKE concert event is after the show when I do a "meet and greet" for families. Dedicated parents stand in line and wait to let their child meet me and hug me and get photos. Over the years I have hugged thousands of little ones, and heard some funny things:

41

👋 "Miss PattyCake — look! I lost a tooth!"

👋 "Are you a real live human person?"

👋 "I have a boo-boo.

👋 "My brother was mean to me."

👋 "How did you get out of my TV?" and this one

👋 "YOU LOOK JUST LIKE MY GRANDMA!"

(Really?! Hat, gloves, costume?

Or am I just that old?)

Sometimes they run to me. Sometimes they are shy. Sometimes they are scared (but not often), and they usually have a story.

This one has stayed with me: A 4-year old girl came slowly toward me. I held out my arms to greet her and said, "Hi there! What is your beautiful name?" She looked at me, wide-eyed and said, "uh … UH … UH … " She turned away and almost screamed, "MOMMY, WHAT'S MY NAME?!"

Do you ever feel that way? So overwhelmed you can hardly remember your own name? Caring for and parenting little ones can be exhausting and terrifying. I don't know about you, but I clearly remember a day I said to myself, "What was I thinking?! I just wanted a baby, but I got a person! And now, I am the one who is responsible for this person!! YIKES!"

KITCHEN HELP

I remember this day in my kitchen: Christopher was probably 10 months old and in the highchair, crying. Marilyn was two and on the floor, loudly banging a wooden spoon on a pan (which I had given her). She was singing and making "music." Usually I encourage this and sing along, but this morning I had HAD IT. The kitchen was a mess — the baby had thrown his food on the floor, and I felt like crying too. I "hit the wall" and did the only thing I knew to do … I yelled, "LORD JESUS!" Well, that shut the kids up. They both were scared, I think. Wide eyed, they looked at their mommy. That didn't stop me. I closed my eyes and kept yelling,

"HELP ME!
I DO NOT KNOW
HOW TO DO THIS!"

You should know I was 34 years old and before *this* had been a professional singer, teacher, on a church staff, worship leader, and had traveled around the world. That was EASY compared to this new job. Now, my husband was at work with our only car. I was stuck in this rental house in a new city, knew very few people and was alone with these children.

The baby cried more. My 2-year old thought my yelling was a new song or game and she joined me! She shouted with me in her little voice, "LORD JESUS, HELP MOMMY!" That was grace to me. I felt the nudge —the quiet *You are trying too hard. Stop, enjoy the moment, take a break.* I took a deep breath, scooped my boy from the high chair, and put him on the floor with me. I gave him a spoon, and the three of us made a racket, banging on pots, making a "joyful noise." (Psalm 100:1) I was crying and laughing, the kids were having fun and eating Cheerios off the floor. And, it didn't bother me one bit. And there was joy in the journey. My friend, Sheila Walsh says, "Jesus lives close to the floor." His name is Emmanuel ... which means 'God with us.'" (Matthew 1:23.)

Not long after that day I was reading my Bible and saw this verse: "Call out for insight and cry aloud for understanding." (Proverbs 2:3)

Next to that verse in my Bible I wrote, I DID THAT! And I had a good laugh. I always think of God watching us, like we watch our children, and smiling — laughing — occasionally slapping an angel and saying, "Did you see that?!"

The story about the little girl who forgot her name has an ending. When she turned to her Mommy and asked, "WHAT'S MY NAME?!," her mother calmly said, "Your name is 'Rebekah' and I am here with you." That spoke volumes to me. We all need reminding our Father knows our name.

Also, He knows what we NEED. Here again is the promise: "God's divine power has granted to us all things that pertain to life and godliness." (2 Peter 1:3; NIV) Read it again—*ALL THINGS*. Another translation reads, "His divine power has given us everything we need for a godly life ... " Jesus said,

"Your father knows the
things you need before you even ask."
(Matthew 6:8) (NIV)

● ●

So let's recap:

God knows our name

God knows what we need

He wants to give us what we need

We have an
ALL ACCESS PASS
through Jesus

Never fear,
Help is near,
All you need
Is a listening ear.

(Hey — I'm **MISS PATTYCAKE**. I rhyme all the time.)

We need to HEAR from God as we care for the children in our lives. We need wisdom! Pray these words with King David, "Hear, O Lord, and be merciful to me; O Lord, be my helper!" Psalm 30:10

Solomon is considered the wisest man who ever lived. He authored Proverbs, Ecclesiastes, Song of Solomon, many Psalms and much is written of his life. In the account of his life, (1 Kings 3:5) the Lord appears to him and says, "Ask for whatever you want me to give you." Solomon asks for "an understanding mind and a discerning heart to govern your people and distinguish between right and wrong." In Hebrew, the word *understanding* is defined as "a hearing ear."

God gives wisdom, knowledge and understanding (hearing ear) to those who ask. (Proverbs 2:6-8, James 1:5)

When I think about the help I need, I remember God told Solomon to ASK.

ASK

We have access to EVERYTHING WE NEED:

• • • • • • • • • • • • • • • • • • •

"God will supply all my needs according to His riches in glory."
Philippians 4:19

• • • • • • • • • • • • • • • • • • •

"Praise be to God ... Who has blessed us in Christ with every spiritual blessing in the heavens."
Ephesians 1:3

● ● ● ● ● ● ● ● ● ● ● ● ● ● ● ● ● ●

"Ask and it will be given to you; seek and you will find; knock and the door will be opened to you."
Matthew 7:7

"Call to Me and I will answer you, and I will tell you great and mighty things, which you do not know."
Jeremiah 33:3

Those are just a very few examples of God's promise to HELP us. And just look at this:

"For I, the LORD, have spoken, and I will do what I say."
Ezekiel 36:36

Whoo hoo! YAY, GOD!! That is a Hallelujah verse! And in case you think you have to "get it all right," "figure it all out," or read your Bible more ... just remember this HUGE TRUTH:

47

"for it is God who works in you both to will and to do His good pleasure." Philippians 2:13

WHEW! It's all God ... working in me and that's good news!

Here's a question ... is caring for, loving, teaching, protecting children part of "His good pleasure?" The answer is, as my children would say, "DUH." Jesus said: "Let the little children come to me, and do not hinder them, for the kingdom of heaven belongs to such as these." Matthew 19:14 (NIV)

When you and I participate in the spiritual formation of these little ones, we are taking part in Kingdom work! I hope that made you smile.

Want more encouragement? Sure you do!

"Be strong and courageous. Do not be afraid; do not be discouraged, for the LORD your God will be with you wherever you go." Joshua 1:9

This verse was on my mirror for years! And when I thought about being "strong and courageous" I remembered God could do strong and courageous work in me and through me! I just need to ask!

WE HAVE ACCESS TO MORE THAN WE KNOW

My pastor, Scotty Smith at Christ Community Church in Franklin, TN, told this story during a sermon. I have never forgotten it (and I've heard LOTS of sermons!):

There was a man who saved and saved for a cruise. He had dreamed for years of traveling on a ship, and he used almost every dime he had to buy the ticket. He was having a wonderful time and enjoying all the sights, but his chair was empty at every meal. Finally, one of the stewards went to his cabin and said, "We have noticed you missed your meals with us for the past few days. Is anything wrong? Can we change the menu for you or get you something special to eat?" "Oh, NO." the man replied. "I only had enough money to pay for my room, and I just can't afford the meals, so I brought along some crackers and cheese, and other snacks. Don't worry about me." Taken aback, the steward said, "Did no one tell you?! All your meals are included in the ticket price. All the food is available to you — at no extra cost. There is a buffet with all you can eat!"

Buffet? BUFFET! NO WAY!

That's right ladies and gentleman — it is "all you can eat," available 24/7. And it is MORE THAN YOU KNOW!

"God is able to do exceedingly abundantly above all we could ask or even think."
Ephesians 3:20

• • • • • • • • • • • • • • • • • • •

"If you, then, though you are evil, know how to give good gifts to your children, how much more will your Father in heaven give good gifts to those who ask him!"
Matthew 7:11 (NIV)

Call me silly, but I remember this is as my 7-11 verse. When I was growing up there weren't as many quick-stop stores … the only one was 7-Eleven® (so named for its hours of operation). This is a "quick-stop" verse. If we need something we can ASK — and BELIEVE, because …

"This is the confidence we have in approaching God: that if we ask anything according to his will, he hears us. And if we know that he hears us — whatever we ask — we know that we have what we asked of him."
1 John 5:14-15

I even have hand motions for this. Ready? Put your hand out, palm up and say, "ASK." (Go on, do it.) Now, make a fist and put it to your chest — yeah, like a Roman salute. Say, "BELIEVE!"

> **"So, what do you think? With God on our side like this, how can we lose? If God didn't hesitate to put everything on the line for us, embracing our condition and exposing himself to the worse by sending his own Son, is there anything else he wouldn't gladly and freely do for us?"**
> Romans 8:31-32

Selah (Hebrew word meaning *pause and think about it.*)

I recently heard a pastor say, "When we are in Christ, we are given a first class ticket but we insist on traveling in coach." WOW, I love first class! I'm not suggesting our lives should be cozy, always cushy, with all the food and drinks you want. Jesus said, "In this life you will have trouble, BUT BE OF GOOD CHEER. I have overcome the world." (John 16:33) *[emphasis added]* Since the "same Spirit that raised Jesus from the dead lives in us" (Romans 8:11), we have ACCESS to that overcoming power which produces JOY in us for the journey through this life! YAY, GOD!

COLORFUL ACCESS

I am a visual learner. I love pictures and I love color! I especially love color pictures. You should see my house. My children say I'm a color junkie.

So, I imagine this picture when I need HELP — and I know where my help comes from. I "see" the Father with His hand on a big lever connected to a bright pink fire hose. Let's say I am having a hard time being nice to someone (I know you can't believe that … I mean, I am that smiley **MISS PATTY-CAKE** woman! Well, believe it.) So here's the picture: I close my eyes and breathe (very important to breathe before you speak) and "see" God calmly walk to the hose labeled KINDNESS. HE WAITS FOR ME TO ASK — then He flips that lever and *WHOOSH*, kindness pours through the hose and right into me. Then, like a pipe, it runs through me and spills out onto that "nasty" someone (who is often my own child)! By the way, how can such small people bring out the worst in us??! UGH. My mother used to say, "No one can bring something out of you that is not already there." I hate hearing that. But it is true and only serves to remind me of my need of HELP.

What an opportunity for God to remind me of the ALL ACCESS PASS we have through Him. Whatever we need … any time … all the time.

Who needs some "color" — some flavor? I like to think of God's HELP in terms of the fruit of the Spirit. This fruit is given to all who believe and receive and is ours for the asking. So, look at this:

"Now the fruit of the Spirit is ... " Galatians 5:22

Did you notice the word *fruit* is singular? There is ONE fruit with many "flavors" — or as I like to think, many colors.

Here is your **ALL ACCESS COLOR PASS** to the fruit:

LOVE	white (pure, clean)
JOY	yellow (sunny, happy)
PEACE	green (a fresh, grassy meadow)
PATIENCE	blue (an ocean, the sky, wide and big)
GENTLENESS	pink (a newborn baby)
KINDNESS	gold (great worth, makes you rich to give or receive)
GOODNESS	orange (juicy, healthy, life-giving vitamin C)
FAITHFULNESS	red (blood brothers who stick together)
SELF CONTROL	purple (royal color — the king of "fruit")

This works for me. Does it help you?

As I write this I am sitting at my kitchen table looking at a fabulous, wildly colorful painting of a royal crown. My friend, Ginnie Johnson from Dallas, is the artist. When I first saw this painting, it nearly took my breath away! Ginnie travels all over, telling women we are the KING'S DAUGHTERS (www.kings-daughters.com). Her work is always signed with this verse, "The King's daughter is all glorious within." (Psalm 45:13) God is coloring our world by His Spirit with all the FRUIT! Let God color you and become all glorious within.

GIGGLE BREAK

A mommy was busy working in her kitchen while her little girl was playing/singing/doing her 3-year old thing. Soon the mommy realized it had gotten quiet. Uh-oh. Nervously, she went to check. She found her darling girl in the bathroom standing by the sink, smearing RED LIPSTICK all over her face. Before the mother could even speak, her daughter said, "Look Mommy, I painted YOU all over ME!"

God wants to paint Himself all over us. He wants to change us into the image of His dear Son, the One who loved us and gave Himself for us. Jesus came to give us "life abundant" (John 10:10), colorful, joyful life. And He will use the children in our world to speed the process along.

A SCARY CAT DAY

It was nearly noon and the trip to the grocery store had taken longer than I wanted. All three of us were cranky. Grocery shopping takes more energy than I ever think it will. And, it really wears out the children! I finally checked out, wrestled them into the car, and drove toward home.

"Mommy, I'm hungry. I'm thirsty, too. How long till we get home? Will it rain today? What color is the moon? Do fish have teeth? Christopher won't be quiet!" (Do questions ever end?!)

Even getting out of the car was a chore! My 10 month-old son was fussing loudly and was heavy on my right arm in the car carrier while my other arm was loaded with grocery bags. "Go straight into the house, please," I instructed 27 month-old Marilyn, who slowly walked up the front porch stairs in front of me. I felt like a shepherd, herding her toward the door. Time for lunch and naps. "Please hurry! Mommy is TIRED."

She suddenly stopped, screamed, and ran to the other end of our wide front porch. There was a kitty near our front door. Not our kitty — a strange kitty— a big, hairy CAT. She was terrified! Speaking soothing words to Marilyn, I walked calmly past the cat to the door.   It looked at me. I looked at it. It didn't move. I unlocked the front door being careful not to drop bags or baby. "Come on, sweetie. Mommy sees the cat. The cat won't get you." I shooed the cat. It lazily walked a few feet from the door. Marilyn was not moving. "Honey, I won't let the cat hurt you."

"The CAT, THE CAT!" she wailed. Holding the door open I said, "The kitty will not hurt you. Just please run on into the house."

"NO, NO, it's a BIG CAT," she whined. Frustrated, I said, "Marilyn, look at me. Don't look at the cat. Walk to ME and come in the house." She didn't move. My arms were aching now. "Please, honey — don't look at the cat. I will not let the cat hurt you. Look at me." I was begging, rather LOUDLY now. The baby was crying and I was on the brink. "SWEET-IE! If that cat comes anywhere near you, I will KICK IT AWAY!"

Finally, after much coaxing, she took a tentative step, looked at me, then the cat, then me, the cat, me, cat, and RAN past me into the house. WHEW! I turned to the cat, stomped my foot and said, "SCAT!" The strange cat flew off our porch. We never saw it again.

Later, I pondered that episode, and had an "AHA" moment. (I hope you have those occasionally.) How like our Father to show me something profound in a typical "mothering" day. A silly cat moment became this lesson: I am that scared little girl — afraid of the "cats" in my life. The Father says, "Look at ME — not the cats. Keep your eyes on ME — I will not let the 'cats' hurt you. Walk the way I will show you. I am a good shepherd, herding you to a safe place. I have set before you an open door. Trust ME. Rely on ME."

WOW. I have found "mothering" to be the place where I learn the most about God's "Fathering." Today, in your mothering, ask the Father to show you how your parenting can reflect His parenting. He is able to KICK THE CAT!

"I will keep him in perfect peace whose mind is stayed on Me, because he trusts in Me."
Isaiah 26:3

"The Lord is my shepherd, I lack nothing … He guides me along the right paths for His name's sake. Even though I walk through the valley of the shadow of 'CATS' I will fear no evil, for He is with me … " Psalm 23:3NIV *[paraphrase mine]*

MASTER KEY

The icon I used for this chapter is a KEY.
The master key giving us ACCESS to God's "ALL" is *prayer*.

Pray? How do we do that? Does that sound complicated? Intimidating? How does it make you feel? Some of us have this idea that prayer can only happen when we are alone, quiet, maybe on our knees, early in the morning, or at the end of the day. When you work with babies and little children, those opportunities are rare, so this thinking might lead you to believe you can't use the MASTER KEY.

Is that what you think? What if prayer is different from what you think? What if prayer can simply be a thought you turn toward the Father at any time? What if you don't even need words? As you know, the children in your care don't always use words to communicate. You know the "I'm hungry" cry, the "I'm angry" or "I'm happy" noises. What a great picture for us! How much more does our Father know us. Sometimes in the routine of caring for children, we don't have words either. That's ok! Look at this, "the Spirit helps us in our weakness. We do not know what we ought to pray for, but the Spirit himself intercedes for us through wordless groans." (Romans 8:26) (NIV)

Prayer can be all day, every day, all the time, anytime. It's easy to chat with someone who knows you well. And who knows you better than anyone? Go ahead, say it … that's right! God, the One who made you, God the One who loves you! Prayer is an ongoing CONVERSATION with the One who loves you and He is always listening.

Max Lucado has written a book called <u>Prayer</u>. In it, after studying prayers all through the Bible, he sums up the essence of a petition in a simple way. Here is Max's "pocket prayer":[22]

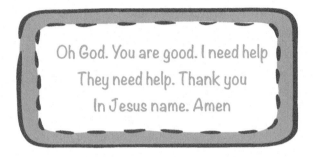

Oh God. You are good. I need help
They need help. Thank you
In Jesus name. Amen

If you don't have time for that many words, here is an even simpler one:

C.S. Lewis is credited with saying, "The prayer God loves to answer is 'help'!"

"God did not spare his own Son, but gave him up for us all, how will He not also with Jesus freely give us ALL THINGS."

Rom 8:32

INFANCY

It's a … *GIRL*! That was a moment I will never forget. My husband and I decided there are too few surprises in life, so we waited until the birth for the big news. She had blue eyes and blond hair! Another surprise, since we are both brown eyed with brown hair. And, what a voice! Man, that baby could cry. "Just like her mother," my husband said. Not the crying, the volume! Her birth was an emotional highpoint in my life. "For this child I prayed, and the Lord has given me what I asked," like Hannah said in 1 Samuel 1:27.

Later I would laugh about this. I just wanted a baby — I mean my friends had babies, I was already past 30, and my parents wanted grands, so I asked God for a baby. What God gave me was a PERSON! So now I have this little person. And, this is not COSTCO — you cannot take her back! Pretty SCARY.

So — how to begin? She didn't come with a manual, for crying out loud! How do I begin this journey of parenting?

Stephen Covey has wisely said, [23]

"Begin with the end in mind."

THE IMPORTANCE OF NOW

We mommies think these days will NEVER END. The diapers, the messy bottoms, feeding and feeding and not sleeping, the crying, the wondering *Is she ok?*, the runny nose, changing her clothes, in the car seat, out of the car seat, trips to the doctor, awake, asleep, do it all again tomorrow.

The wise Erma Bombeck said this about motherhood:[24]

We go about our daily routine, stringing one brightly colored wooden bead after another, feeling pretty proud of ourselves. We assume we're accomplishing so much, but the illusion of productivity is shattered when, at the end of the day, we look down at our necklace only to discover that there is no knot. The once-strung beads are now scattered all over the place, and we have to start all over.

This thought is echoed in *What Every Mom Needs* by Elisa Morgan & Carol Kuykendall:[25]

When do moms get to finish anything? We can't finish a meal without getting up and running to the stove, or the refrigerator, or to answer the phone. We scarcely finish a thought before somebody needs something and we've lost our concentration. The very job of mothering (caregiving) is unending."

In those early days I slept little, read all the books I had, called my mom every day, listened to all the advice anyone gave, and it seemed every hour brought a discovery — velvet soft skin, perfect hand curled around my finger, tiny sharp fingernails, listening for any sound, nursing her, dressing her, changing her, watching her little face in wonder, amazed by her breathing and tiny heartbeat. It was fascinating and terrifying at the same time. What if I dropped and broke her? What if I ate something wrong and made her sick? What if I slept through a feeding? What if ... ?????? Can you guess what my one word prayer was? Say it with me ... "HELP!"

The day came to take her for those dreaded shots. I remember it well. I carefully got her into the car seat and drove like a snail to the doctor. It was traumatic ... FOR ME. That perfect trusting face was looking around peacefully until she felt the needle, then this slow-motion transformation as she realized … PAIN. She cried. I cried. (Have you been there?) It was awful. The nurse looked at my tears, patted my knee and said, "Don't worry, honey. The mommies always cry more than the babies."

Very late that night I was awake nursing and changing her, when I rolled her over and OH NO, touched that tender spot on her hip from the vaccination. Out came her loud cry! I was devastated. I didn't mean to hurt her. She cried, I cried again and then began talking to her (as if she could understand me) "I'M SORRY! Oh, sweet baby, I am sorry you are in pain. I didn't want to hurt you, but you needed those shots and they are good for you and you will never be sick with those diseases and believe me if there was any other way …" I kept on talking until she calmed down and I stopped crying. And then — a MOMENT when God "helped" me. An obscure verse popped into my head:

> "I am about to do something
> in your day you would not have believed,
> even if I had told you …"
> Habakkuk 1:5

WOW! There I was weeping over my child's pain, trying to explain it to her, knowing she could not understand my words, and God had said the same thing! He is "about to do something" that you cannot understand or believe, EVEN IF HE TOLD YOU.

That night I got something new — something MORE. That scripture was, to me, a revelation of God's watchful caring, and I got it — He sees me, knows my pain, and wants me to trust His kind intention even when I don't understand. That was a "page-turning day" for me. I knew God loved me, and wanted me to know Him, but something more — I now knew a mother's love, which ushered me into a new depth of "knowing" the Father. Also, I knew it was my JOB to teach this little PERSON about THAT God — the Father — and the time to start was NOW, before she could even understand.

This is not a new idea[26] ...

> You know that the beginning is the most important part of any work, especially in the care of a young and tender thing; for that is the time at which the character is being formed and the desired impression is more readily taken.
> –Plato's Republic

Child expert and author Jeanne Hendricks has said:[27]

> *To the newborn child, people are everything. The earliest social skill is when that little infant can find and hold the eyes of an adult in what we call the 'quiet-alert' stage … It's when that little one looks at you and says, 'Can I trust you?' Because the first developmental task of a newborn child is to find out, 'Is this a safe world? Am I going to be accepted and loved?'*

Most parents and caregivers think about these things:

? Food: breast, bottle or combination?

? Should I use a pacifier?

? Do I have the right colors for stimulation?

? Am I talking enough/too much to her?

? How should I exercise those little arms and legs?

? Do I have the right music for helping synapses connect?

? What will help her stop crying?

? Does she have an allergy?

? Is she mentally and emotionally normal?

Have you driven yourself, and others, CRAZY talking about, researching, and trying to get it all 'right'?! Probably.

As important as a baby's diet and exercise for physical development, stimulation for mental and emotional development, who is talking to you about their spiritual development?

SPIRITUAL FORMATION

Would you like to know what God has to say about this? ME TOO! This verse helped solidify my purpose as a new mother, and later as **MISS PATTYCAKE**.

"FROM INFANCY you have known
the holy Scriptures, which are able
to make you wise unto salvation
through faith in Jesus Christ our Lord."
2 Timothy 3:15
[emphasis mine]

This is what I like about that verse ... it references the life of young Timothy. Seldom in the Bible are we given the names of caregivers, but with Timothy, we know who they were: his mother and grandmother, Lois and Eunice. Both of these women took the time and made the effort to sing, speak and teach little Timothy the Word of God.

There is not a lot of information in Scripture regarding Lois and Eunice, but what we do know should be an encouragement to all mothers who want to teach their children to know God. Lois and Eunice were a mother/daughter team who parented Timothy. He later became the Apostle Paul's most trusted companion and disciple.

It is only in Acts 1:6 and 2 Timothy 1:5 that we find record of these women, but what a strong commendation the Apostle Paul gives to them. In 2 Timothy 1:5, Paul writes: "I have been reminded of your sincere faith, which first lived in your grandmother Lois and in your mother Eunice and, I am persuaded, now lives in you also." These women were responsible for passing their faith on to the next generation.

The family lived at Lystra, and it is likely that during Paul's first visit to that city that Lois, Eunice, and Timothy were all converted to the Christian faith. There is no doubt that their devout Jewish faith and knowledge of the Old Testament Scriptures prepared their hearts to hear the words of Paul regarding eternal life through Jesus Christ.

The compelling feature of the Scriptural record of Eunice and Lois is their religious influence on Timothy. Since his father is not mentioned in connection with Timothy's faith, it is apparent that these two godly women were the ones who trained him up so that he both knew and loved

God's word. The name Timothy means "one who fears God," a name obviously picked by his faithful mother. Grandmother and mother had no doubt been the teachers of his youth. His fitness to be Paul's companion and co-worker finds its explanation largely in the home training and pious example given him by these two noble women. It was from them also that the young Timothy derived his first impressions of Christian truth; for Paul calls to remembrance the earnest faith which first dwelt in them.

The record of Timothy demonstrates the value of positive Christian training in the home. Lois and Eunice took the responsibility to pass on their faith very seriously and as a result they raised up a young man to become a servant of Christ. For this, they have gone down in history as outstanding mothers and great women of faith.[28]

Remember what Stephen Covey said: "Begin with the END in mind."[29]

What is the end? I hope you, like Lois and Eunice, want the "end" to be-a vital, authentic relationship with God the Father through Jesus, empowered by the Holy Spirit. THAT is what starting early can do. When we pour into little lives the LOVE of God and the WORD of God, it is "able to make [our children] wise unto salvation." (2 Timothy 3:16) I love *The Message* translation of this verse:

"Stick with what you have learned —
why, you took in the sacred Scriptures with
your mother's milk! There's nothing like the
written Word of God for showing you the way
to salvation through faith in Christ Jesus."

• • • • • • • • • • • • • • • • • •

Proverbs 22:6 says,
"Start children off on the way they should go,
and even when they are old they will not turn from it."
(NIV)

"Point your kids in the right direction —
when they are old they wont' be lost."
(*The Message*)

GET STARTED EARLY!

Billy Graham said, "The greatest surprise in life to me is the brevity of life."[30]

Even when you think these early years are going on and on and wonder, *When will this child ever be potty trained*, remember this: you will be surprised, looking back, how quickly they have grown.

Don't put it off! Don't think spiritual formation is someone else's job. Don't think, *I take them to church, what more can*

I do? Even if they cannot understand your WORDS, they do soak in LIFE. Because "the word of God is alive and active." (Hebrews 4:12)

I have discovered, especially working with special needs children, that even when all the synapses don't connect correctly, and they don't always understand our words, there is a deeper understanding and knowing that is absorbed.

There is a planting of LIFE that happens when we speak and SING the living Word of God to our babies!

Do you wonder, as I did, if all the effort we are making in the early months and years really matters? Will they remember the songs, the activities, the stories? It is an understandable concern. What we do know is this, without a firm foundation, a structure cannot stand. The foundation is underground and often unseen. But without it, a structure falls. Jesus told the story of a house built on sand and compared that to a house built on a rock. Which house stood? What you are helping develop in little lives is a foundation upon which they can stand. YOUR LABOR IS NOT IN VAIN!

> **"It is the same with my word.
> I send it out, and it always produces fruit.
> It will accomplish all I want it to."**
>
> Isaiah 55:11

It's even better in *The Message*:

"So will the words that come out of my mouth
not come back empty-handed.
They'll do the work I sent them to do,
they'll complete the assignment I gave them."

Infants are sponges. They soak up whatever touches them. Give them plenty of "washing by the water of the Word of God." (Ephesians 5:26). It is "living" water (Hebrews 4:12) and will nourish their spirits. You can trust God will use what you invest in little lives.

GIGGLE BREAK

A 3-year old raptly watched his mother nurse his new baby sister. As he looked on, he innocently asked, "What comes out of those nozzles?" Smiling, his mother said, "It's milk." He then asked, "Is one hot and one cold, or is one white and one chocolate?"

SEVEN WAYS TO PRACTICE PRAISE

Early in my life I discovered the power of PRAISE. It is a big, fat word, which is always a verb, and we will unpack it later in this chapter.

Let's begin with this truth: When we turn our attention to God and give Him THANKS AND PRAISE, it changes US. When we tell Him who He IS, He reminds us who WE ARE. We are His children, heirs to all the promises. He empowers us — and, let's face it, we need HELP!

This is the way it began for me. I was a college student studying music. A vocal performance major, I loved opera, musical theater and show choir. I dreamed of singing in New York or on a cruise ship, or just anywhere on stage!

Enter Jesus. He took center stage in my life and began to change me. His words encouraged me to "Sing, sing your hearts out to God." (Colossians 3:17, *The Message*)

"Sing songs from your heart to Christ. Sing praises over everything, any excuse for a song to God the Father in the name of our Master, Jesus Christ." (Ephesians 5:19-20) And the big one for me: "He has put a NEW SONG in my mouth, a song of PRAISE to our God." (Psalm 40:3) *[emphasis mine]*

At that time I wasn't completely sure what all those verses meant. Oh sure, I had sung plenty of hymns and classical music with the words, "Praise God." Every Sunday of my life we sang the "Doxology" (taken from Psalm 150). But just what was this "new song" God was telling me to sing? THAT was the right question. It was the question which launched my journey toward what God wanted to do with the music He had given me.

Quickly, I discovered this:

PRAISE IS THE PATHWAY
INTO HIS PRESENCE

Psalm 100:4 says, "Enter His gates with thanksgiving and His courts with praise." A quick look at the layout of the temple or the tabernacle of David shows us this geography or floor plan. You must walk through the gates to even get into the area where sacrifice and cleansing took place. To come into the place of His presence, where He IS by His Spirit, we must enter His COURTS. Only the priests were allowed to enter the courts. But now, because of Jesus, we are all priests and can "enter His courts with praise."

Psalm 22:3 confirms this:

"God is holy and dwells where the praises of His people are offered."

● ● ● ● ● ● ● ● ● ● ● ● ● ● ● ● ● ● ● ●

Psalm 16:11says,

" ... in His presence is fullness of JOY."

● ● ● ● ● ● ● ● ● ● ● ● ● ● ● ● ● ● ● ●

And in Psalm 34:5:

"Those who look to Him are radiant."

● ● ● ● ● ● ● ● ● ● ● ● ● ● ● ● ● ● ● ●

Because of this revelation, I began to sing PRAISES to God — and I was changed! YAHOO! Truly, it is a "GOOD THING to give thanks to God and to SING HIS PRAISE." (Psalm 92:1, [*emphasis mine*] Not only that — there is

MORE! Isaiah 61:3 says this: "I will give them a garment of praise instead of a heavy, burdened, and failing spirit." (Amplified Version)

That is GOOD NEWS! The truth of this changed my life then and still energizes me today! This energy is something WE ALL NEED!!

As followers of Jesus, we need to know WHO we are, WHAT we are to do, and HOW to live in the presence of God because "times of refreshing come from the presence of the Lord." (Acts 3:19) And how do we get into the presence of the Lord? GOOD QUESTION! The Bible says, "God inhabits (lives in) the PRAISES of his people." (Psalm 22:3) The Hebrew word used for "praises" in that verse means to SING!

Sing? Wow — what a concept! As MISS PATTYCAKE, I love to encourage parents and caregivers to ...

SING YOUR WAY THROUGH YOUR DAY!

There are other ways to give God praise, and we will look at those, but this is so important to know: MUSIC IS "MAGIC." It is the fastest, most permanent way to get information into our minds. Especially effective is music designed to teach about God's "great big world," God's character, Bible stories. It can also create an atmosphere and language for giving Him thanks and praise in an age appropriate way.

So before I get too excited about the HOW TO part of praising God, let's begin with the WHAT.

WHAT IS PRAISE?

This was my question when I felt urged by God to embrace this verse for my life: "He has put a new song in my heart, it is a song of praise," (Psalm 40:3) and this translation, "He taught me how to sing the latest God-song, a praise-song to our God." (*The Message*)

Over the years I have done quite a lot of reading and studying about "praise" and this is my favorite definition:[31]

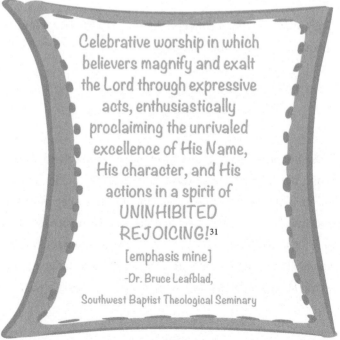

Celebrative worship in which believers magnify and exalt the Lord through expressive acts, enthusiastically proclaiming the unrivaled excellence of His Name, His character, and His actions in a spirit of UNINHIBITED REJOICING![31]
[emphasis mine]
-Dr. Bruce Leafblad,
Southwest Baptist Theological Seminary

The PRAISE of man toward God is the means by which we express our joy to the Lord. We are commanded to PRAISE God both for WHO He is and for WHAT He does (Psalm150:2). Praising God for who He is is called ADORATION; praising Him for WHAT HE DOES is known as THANKSGIVING. Praise of God may be in song or prayer, individually or collectively, spontaneous or prearranged; originating from the emotions or from the will.[32]

-<u>Illustrated Bible Dictionary</u>

WHAT IS WORSHIP?

We hear much these days about worship. We go to *worship service*. We sing *praise and worship* songs. Since "praise" is always biblically defined as something we DO, what is "worship?" This calls for definition and clarification.

The word "worship" has Anglo Saxon roots and comes from "worth-ship" which speaks of the value placed on someone or something. When we value someone, we demonstrate it with gifts/time/thanks.

"Worship" in the Greek is *PROSKYNEO*: "to come near and kiss (the hand), denotes reverence and humility, to prostrate oneself before."

WORSHIP is the whole of life. It's not that
we fit worship into our lives, but we fit our
lives into worship. Worship is the process of
getting nearer to our God.
If we think that worship is just a time of
singing, we have missed it. Worship is the
overflow of our ever-
deepening relationship with God, and that
embraces the whole of life, not just a couple
of hours on a Sunday.[33]

-Graham Kendrick

When we "worship" (value, honor, come near to) we will sense God's enjoyment of us and our enjoyment of Him. "For the Lord takes pleasure in His people; He crowns them with victorious salvation." (Psalm 149:4)

The Westminster Shorter Catechism asks these questions:[34]

Q. 1. What is the chief end of man?

A. Man's chief end is to glorify God, and to enjoy him forever.

Q. 2. What rule hath God given to direct us how we may glorify and enjoy him?

A. The Word of God, which is contained in the Scriptures of the Old and New Testaments is the only rule to direct us how we may glorify and enjoy him.

GLORIFY AND ENJOY = WORSHIP!

SO, since worship is our goal, our purpose, our destiny, how do we worship? Psalm 100:4 is the simplest instuction I know: "Enter His gates with THANKSGIVING, and His courts with PRAISE."

Praise is a decision. Praise is always a VERB. It is something we DO. Praise escorts us into His presence, where we WORSHIP, KNOW, and ENJOY HIM. I love this quote:[35]

Praise is the golden bridge to the heart of God.
-Catherine Marshall

WHY PRAISE?
(A QUICK BIBLE LOOK)

We are created for praise.
(Isaiah 43:21, Ephesians 1:13-14)

We are commanded to praise.
(Psalm 113:1, Psalm 150)

We are called to praise.
(1 Peter 2:5-9)

Before we are called to be preachers, teachers, missionaries, or servants (or parents/caregivers) in any way, we are called to WORSHIP as PRIESTS! 1 Peter 2:5-9 tells us, "We are a chosen generation, a royal priesthood, a holy nation — a people belonging to God, that we declare the praises of Him who has called us out of darkness and into His marvelous light!"

REASONS FOR PRAISE

 God inhabits (lives in) — Psalm 22:3

 God speaks — Psalm 68:32-33,
      Psalm 25:14

 Praise refines US — Proverbs 27:21

 Glorifies God — Psalm 50:23

 Generates Power — Psalm 84, Psalm 149,
      Psalm 8:2

 Precedes Victory — 2 Chronicles 20

 Purpose of People — Isaiah 43:21

So, are you convinced yet? Are you thinking, "Wow, this sounds pretty powerful?" Well, you should be! It is ALL THAT! Psalm 107:8: "Oh that men would PRAISE the Lord … " This is the our "high priestly" calling. And here is something even more profound: In the courts of the temple of Jerusalem there hung a four-inch thick curtain, separating the people from the Holy Place where the Presence of God lived. When Jesus died, that curtain was torn apart, top to bottom, by God Himself, to show we now have ALL access to His presence. (Remember our ALL ACCESS PASS?) That put an end to the bloody sacrifices God had required for 2000 years. Jesus changed everthing! He gave us "boldness, full freedom and confidence to enter into the holy place by His blood, by this fresh (new) and living way which he initiated and dedicated and opened for us, through the veil, that is to say, His flesh." (Hebrews 10:19-20) So now, as priests (and remember we all are priests (1 Peter 2:9), we have a NEW JOB! Here it is:

> "Through Him (Jesus) then let us continue to offer up the sacrifice of praise, that is the fruit of our lips giving thanks to His name."
>
> Hebrews 13:15

I love *The Message* translation: "Let's take our place outside with Jesus, no longer pouring out the sacrificial blood of animals but pouring out sacrificial praises from our lips to God in Jesus' name."

So — are you ready to get started?? Lemme hear you say, "YAY!"

HOW TO PRACTICE PRAISE

Here are, in order, the seven most often used Hebrew words translated into English as "praise":[36]

1. HALAL: "to be clear, shine, boast, rave, laud, celebrate, dance, leap, to be clamorously foolish, with reckless abandon!"

WHOO HOO! My favorite word, *Hallelujah,* comes from *HALAL.* And everywhere you see *Hallelujah* written in the Bible, it is followed by an exclamation point! In English grammar, this is called an imperative ... a command! I love to encourage people to repent, to change their thinking, change their minds about praising God. It is NOT AN OPTION. It is something we MUST DO! And, when we HALLELUJAH (*HALAL* to God), we put ourselves in position to receive from God! Oh, this is soooo good.

Here is a "fatter" definition of HALAL:

"to express great [in an extreme degree] or extravagant [spending much more than is necessary; excessive; exceeding the bounds of reason; going beyond what is justifiable; unrestrained] admiration [to regard with wonder, pleasure, approval]."

In the following verses, HALAL is translated in these English words:

A. **Praise:** I Chronicles 16:4; 23:5, 30; 25:3; II Chronicles 8:14; 20:19,21 (1st); 23:13; 29:30; 31:2; Psalms 22:22,23, 26; 35:18; 56:4,10 (both); 63:5; 69:30,34; 74:21; 102:18; 104:35; 106:1,48; 107:32; 111:1; 112:1; 113:1 (all); 113:9; 115:17,18; 116:19; 117:1,2; 119:164,175; 135:1 (all), 3,21; 145:2; 146:1 (both),2 (1st),10;

147:1 (1st), 12,20; 148 (all); 149:1,3,9; 150 (all);
Jeremiah 20:13; 31:7; Joel 2:26

B. **Praised:** II Samuel 22:4; I Chronicles 16:25,36;
23:5; II Chronicles 5:13; 7:6; 30:21; Psalms 18:3;
48:1; 96:4; 113:3; 145:3

C. **Praises:** II Chronicles 29:30

D. **Praising:** II Chronicles 5:13

E. **Glory:** I Chronicles 16:10; Psalms 105:3; 106:5;
Isaiah 41:16; Jeremiah 4:2; 9:24

F. **Boast:** Psalms 34:2; 44:8

2. YADAH: "to worship with extended hands, to throw out the hands giving thanks to God, lifting hands in surrender, commending a blessing with hands. This is the opposite of wringing the hands." II Chronicles 7:6; 20:21; Psalms 7:17, 9:1; 28:7; 30:9; 33:2; 42:5; 42:11; 43:4; 43:5; 44:8-45:17; 49:18; 52:9; 54:6; 67:3; 67:55; 71:22; 76:10; 86:12; 88:10; 89:5; 99:3; 107:8, 15, 21, 31; 108:3; 109:30; 111:1; 118:19, 21-28,;119:7; 138:2; 145:10; Isaiah 12:1.

Jesus always used stories and examples so people would have mental pictures to better understand His teachings. This idea is not new, and *YADAH* is one of those pictures. When we lift our hands we say, in essence, "I see you for who you are, high and lifted up, and I place myself beneath you." Also, we remind ourselves we are His children. A little child rarely comes to us for love or for help without holding arms up to receive. As a gesture of respect or commendation, we hold up our arms, like a salute. Picture an army, a concert, or any sports event. That is *YADAH*.

FUNNY STORY: I was learning about this hand raising thing when I was in college. While at home one weekend, I was telling my mother about all I was learning … about how it is God's command and lifting hands is a picture of surrender and childlikeness, and on and on. She said, "Honey, that is just so sweet and I'm glad you can do that. I am just not comfortable. That would feel so strange and awkward to me." So I just shut up about it and waited on God since I figured if it was important for her to raise her hands, then God would show her.

Well, here's what happened: She and my dad came down to Auburn University (where I attended as had they) for a football game. The band played! The eagle flew! The crowd yelled! And the head cheerleader came out for the traditional chant and said into the microphone, "Alright eveybody! Get your hands up for a big WAR EAGLE!" (It's an Auburn thing.) So 80,000 people raised their hands. And so did my mom (giggle). She later told me she sensed the Lord ask, *What are you doing?* And she thought, *Well, I'm doin' a WAR EAGLE!* And the Lord said, *So it's ok for you to raise your hands to a football team, but not to Me?* You should see my momma today.

Every Sunday she sits in her big ole' Presbyterian church and raises her hands in front of God and everybody!

3. BARAK (BARAUCH): "to kneel, bless, salute, bow as an act of adoration, or humble submission." Job 1:21; Psalm 96:2; 103:1-2, 20-22; 106:48

The following English words are translated from the Hebrew word BARAK:

A. **Bless:** Psalms 16:7; 66:8; 100:4; 103:1,2,20-22; 104:1,35; 135:19; 135:20

B. **Blessed:** Exodus 18:10; Ruth 4:14; I Samuel 25:32, 39; II Samuel 18:28; I Kings 1:48; 5:7; 8:15,56; 10:9; I Chronicles 16:36; II Chronicles 2:12; 6:4; 9:8; 20:26; Ezra 7:27; Nehemiah 8:6; Psalms 18:46; 31:21; 41:13; 66:20; 68:19,35; 72:18,19; 89:52; 106:48; 119:12; 124:6; 135:21; 144:1; Ezekiel 3:12; Daniel 2:20; 3:28; 4:34.

C. **Kneel:** Psalms 95:6

In Scripture, we are instructed to *bless* (Barauch) the Father:

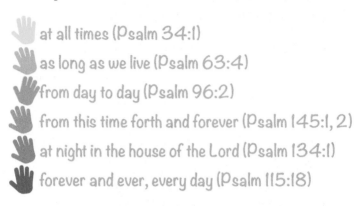

at all times (Psalm 34:1)

as long as we live (Psalm 63:4)

from day to day (Psalm 96:2)

from this time forth and forever (Psalm 145:1, 2)

at night in the house of the Lord (Psalm 134:1)

forever and ever, every day (Psalm 115:18)

I had the privilege of visiting Jerusalem a few years ago. At the Western Wall I watched the many men who prayed there and noticed their posture. Most held their Bibles or prayer books, faced the wall, and bowed as they prayed. This is the idea of BARAUCH.

4. TEHILLAH: "to sing with, by, or in the Spirit, the singing of HALALS."

TEHILLAH is only translated in English as:

Praise: I Chronicles 16:35; II Chronicles 20:22; Nehemiah 9:5; 12:46; Psalm 9:14; 22:3,25; 33:1; 34:1; 35:28; 40:3; 48:10; 51:15; 65:1; 66:2,8; 71:6,8,14; 79:13; 100:4; 102:21; 106:2,12,47; ii 1:10; 119:171; 145; Title, 21; 147:1(2nd); 148:14(1st); 149:1(2nd); Exodus 15:11; Deuteronomy 10:21; Isaiah 61:3.

If you know me, or have ever seen MISS PATTYCAKE, you can see how committed I am to *TEHILLAH*. Remember my encouragement to "Sing your way through your day?" That's because *TEHILLAH* puts us in the presence of God. Psalm 22:3 says, "God inhabits [lives in] the *TEHILLAH* of his people." When we are where God lives, we are in His Presence. "Times of refreshing come from the presence of the Lord." (Acts 3:19) I don't know about you, but I want to live like that. HALLELUJAH!

5. ZAMAR: "to touch the strings, playing instruments, to make music accompanied by the voice. To celebrate. To sing songs of praise with instruments."

"It is good to give *Yadah* to the Lord, and to *Zamar* to Your Name, O Most High: To declare Your loving kindness in the morning, and Your faithfulness every night. On an instrument, on the strings, on the lute, and on the harp, with harmonious sound." Psalm 92:1-3

"Sing to the Lord with *Towdah*; *Zamar* on the harp to our God ..." Psalm 147:7

"*Zamar* to the Lord with the harp, with the harp and the sound of a psalm, with trumpets and the sound of a horn; Shout joyfully before the Lord, the King." Psalm 98:5, 6

"*Barauch* to the Lord my Rock, who trains my hands for war, and my fingers for battle ... I will sing a new song to You, O God; On a harp of strings I will *Zamar* to You." Psalm 144:1, 9

ZAMAR is translated as:
  A. **Praise:** Psalm 57:7; 108:1; 138:1
  B. **Sing Praises:** Psalm 9:11; 18:49; 27:6; 47:6 (all), 7; 92:1; 108:3; 135:3; 144:9; 146:2; 147:1; 149:3
  C. **Sing:** Psalm 30:4,12; 33:2; 57:9; 59:17; 61:8; 66:2, 4 (both); 71:22, 23; 75:9; 98:4, 5; Isaiah 12:5
  D. **Sing Psalms:** Psalm 105:2

More: 1Chronicles 16:9; Psalm 57:8-9, 7:17, 61:8, 66:2-4, 135:3, 98:5, 9:2, 150.

6. SHABACH: "to proclaim in a loud voice, shout, commend, bless, declare. A loud adoration, the testimony of what God has done-a joyful to overflowing attitude."

This word for "shout" is translated "praise" and "extol" and "commend" in the following verses: Psalm 63:3, 117:1, 145:4, 106:47, 47:1, 100:1, 147:12

Over and over again we are told to shout, to be loud:

"But let all those rejoice who put their trust
in You; let them ever shout for joy, because
You defend them; let those also who love Your
name be joyful in You."

Psalm 5:11

• • • • • • • • • • • • • • • • • •

"Be glad in the Lord and rejoice
you righteous; and shout for joy,
all you upright in heart."

Psalm 32:11

• • • • • • • • • • • • • • • • • •

"Oh clap your hands, all you peoples! Shout
to God with the voice of triumph!"

Psalm 17:1

• • • • • • • • • • • • • • • • • •

"For the Lord has chosen Zion (we, the
church are Zion); He has desired it for His
dwelling place: "This is My resting place
forever; here I will dwell, for I have desired
it. I will abundantly bless her provision; I will
satisfy her poor with bread. I will also clothe
her priests with salvation, and her saints shall
shout aloud for joy."

Psalm 132:13-16

A great example of *SHABACH* is found in Ezra 3:10-13 which says:

"When the builders laid the foundation of the temple of the Lord, the priests stood in their apparel with trumpets, and the Levites, the sons of Asaph, with cymbals, to praise the Lord, according to the ordinance of David King of Israel. And they sang responsively, praising and giving thanks to the Lord: For He is good, for His mercy endures forever toward Israel. Then all the people shouted with a great shout, when they praised the Lord, because the foundation of the house of the Lord was laid."

YAHOO! I love *SHABACH*! And so do children. When I do live events, I always give them permission to use their "outside voices." There is POWER in shouting. When someone shouts you know they mean business. Jesus shouted in righteous anger at the merchants in the temple. The word *shabach* is like the word *halal* and is often written with an exclamation point. That makes it a command!

7. TODAH (TOWDAH): "to extend the hands in a sacrifice of praise, thanksgiving, or thank-offering. Also, to thank in advance for things not yet visible: a faith praise."

   A. **Praise:** Psalm 42:4; 50:23; Jeremiah 17:26, 33:11
   B. **Praises:** Psalm 56:12; 68:4, 32; 75:9
   C. **Thanks:** Nehemiah 12:31, 38, 40
   D. **Thanksgiving:** Leviticus 22:29; Psalm 26:7; 50:14; 69:30; 95:2; 107:22; 116:17; 147:7; Isaiah 51:3; Jeremiah 90:19; Amos 4:5

This faith praise moves God. "He who sacrifices thank-offerings (*TODAH*) honors me and he prepares the way so that I may show him my salvation of God." (Psalm 50:23)

Praise *(TODAH)* prepares the way for deliverance. Check this out: "But I, with shouts of grateful praise *(TODAH)*, will sacrifice to you ... Salvation comes from the Lord. And the Lord commanded the fish and it vomited Jonah onto dry land." Jonah 2:9-10

Other uses of *TODAH*: Jeremiah 17:26; 33:11; Psalm 42:4; 50:14, 56:12, 95:2

MIX IT UP

One of the first verses I remember learning as a child, probably in Vacation Bible School (thank you Dawson Memorial Baptist in Birmingham, Alabama) was Psalm 100. It is entitled "A Psalm for Giving Thanks" and uses an interesting combination of Hebrew words for praise in verse 4: "Enter into his gates with thanksgiving (TODAH) and into his courts with praise (TEHILLAH): give thanks (YADAH) to him and praise (BARAUCH) his name."

 You may be thinking, *That works for you since you dress in that costume and you are naturally uninhibited and you probably didn't grow up in a quiet, conservative*

church like I did. Are you thinking that? Then perhaps you will be encouraged by these words from the great conservative reformer, John Calvin, [37]

"The stability of the world depends on this rejoicing of God in His works. If on earth, such praise of God does not come to pass, ... then the whole order of nature will be thrown into confusion. We are cold when it comes to rejoicing in God! Hence, we need to exercise ourselves in it and employ all our senses in it - our feet, our hands, our arms and all the rest - that they all might serve in the worship of God and so magnify Him. "

Exercise yourself and your children in the PRAISE OF GOD! Now you know there are many ways to give God praise, and He is please with ALL OF THEM! It's okay! There are many ways to give God praise! And He is pleased with all of them. Now that you know more about praise, you may find yourself enjoying NEW expressions of praise to God in your own life.

CHILD-LIKE PRAISE

Have you noticed how easy it is for children to sing/shout/dance/clap/jump/repeat? Are you jealous? I AM! Children are generally uninhibited. They do not overthink. I see this all the time as MISS PATTYCAKE. I have observed there is no need for great logic or apologetics with little children when you talk about God; you just have to tell them His name.

Simply say, "Jesus. The One you can't see. The One who made you and loves you." Often they say, "Oh, Him!"

How can they know this so early?

Ecclesiastes 3:11 says, "God has planted eternity in the human heart." The Amplified Version further explains: "eternity — a divinely implanted sense of a purpose working through the ages which nothing under the sun but God alone can satisfy."

Note also, the great Blaise Pascal wrote a collection of thoughts on theology and philosophy (Pensées)to his skeptical and restless friends. He hoped to move them to seek God. He said, "There is a God shaped vacuum in the heart of every man which cannot be filled by any created thing, but only by God, the Creator, made known through Jesus."[35]

We can begin early to
fill that vacuum with the
Word of God and with His PRAISES!

● ● ● ● ● ● ● ● ● ● ● ● ● ● ● ● ● ●

"Out of the mouths of babes and infants,
God has ordained PRAISE!"
Psalm 8:2 [emphasis mine]

● ● ● ● ● ● ● ● ● ● ● ● ● ● ● ● ● ●

"Nursing infants gurgle choruses about You.
And toddlers shout the songs that drown out enemy
talk, and silence atheistic babble."
(*The Message*)

● ● ● ● ● ● ● ● ● ● ● ● ● ● ● ● ● ● ●

PULLING PRESCHOOLERS INTO PRAISE

P = PRAY ask God for HELP.

U = UNDERSTANDING Now that you have read this chapter, you know better what praise is and how to practice praise with your children.

L = LEVEL Try to think on their level. Remember they have to crawl before walking, and walk before running. They need milk before meat. So, find simple, age appropriate songs, stories, and activities that teach and practice PRAISE. (www.misspattycake.com ... hint, hint)

L = LOVE We already feel love for the children in our care, but love is also a verb ... something we DO. We love God by praising, thanking, obeying, serving Him. Jesus asked Peter, "Do you love me? Feed my lambs." YOU are loving God and loving your children when you PRACTICE PRAISE with them!

Are you ready to "get some praise on," to trade your burdens, your frustration, and your fear for some JOY? After reading this chapter, you will have learned something new. My experience of teaching these biblical truths about PRAISE for more than 30 years has proven that this knowledge is POWERFUL. Hosea 4:6 says, "My people perish from a lack of knowledge." Today, you have armed yourself with life-giving knowledge from the Word of God which can empower you to understand and practice a life of PRAISE.

ENTHUSIASTIC ENJOYMENT

MISS PATTYCAKE rounded a corner at Prestonwood Baptist Church in Dallas and almost bumped into a three year old boy. He looked up at me and screamed! (I'm used to this.) Assuming he was afraid of me in a costume, I dropped to one knee and said, "Hi there!" with a big smile. He backed up a little, never taking his eyes off me and said loudly,

"HOW DID YOU GET OUT OF MY TV?!"
I fell over laughing. I love my job!

> In every job that must be done
> There is an element of fun
> You find the fun and SNAP,
> the job's a game [39]

Did you picture Mary Poppins? Did you hear Julie Andrews in your head as you read? Did you sing it? I always do! She was my childhood hero. I wanted to BE her — mostly just to sing all those songs and jump into the sidewalk picture. Oh, and ride those carousel horses, and dance with Bert, and LAUGH!! I LOVE TO LAUGH! Then I wanted to feed the birds, and fall asleep to the song, "Stay Awake." Then I'd sing "SUPERCALIFRAGALISTICEXPEALIDOSHUS" and "Fly a Kite!"

You know what I love about that movie? There is a variety, a "diet" in the music and the story — fast, slow, sweet, silly, a little scary, working songs, love songs. We are emotional creatures, multi-faceted, and we can be touched by and learn from all sorts of experiences. GOD, our Creator, in whose image we are made, is also multi-faceted. LOOK AROUND! I love what Romans 1:20 says about Him: "Ever since the creation of the world, God's invisible nature and His eternal power have been clearly seen through what has been made."

MISS PATTYCAKE sings this song:[40]

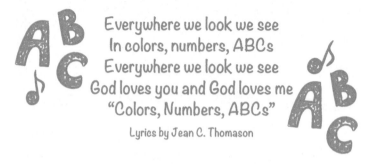

Everywhere we look we see
In colors, numbers, ABCs
Everywhere we look we see
God loves you and God loves me
"Colors, Numbers, ABCs"

Lyrics by Jean C. Thomason

We look, we smell, we taste, we touch, we hear, and we experience the varied "diet" of God's creativity!

GOD AND GROCERIES

I like to EAT, which means I COOK, and therefore … I must GROCERY SHOP. I don't hate the grocery store (especially when they give samples). The relaxing music at my favorite store always slows me down, and so I look at people around me. Lately, I have seen more and more mommies who do this:

Walk in … child on hip or by the hand … pull out cart … plunk child in cart … reach into purse or diaper bag for phone or iPad or any device with a screen … touch "ON" … give device to child … shopping … no talking.

Have you seen this? Do you DO this? Believe me, I get it! We are busy! We have stuff to do, meals to cook, clothes to wash, meetings to attend, calls to make, gotta get through the grocery list, match the coupons, check out, save money, get home ASAP, go, go, GO!

WAIT! This is an opportunity, a creative time to talk to your children about the Lord! Deuteronomy 6:7 says to talk about Him when you sit at home, when you walk along the road, get up in the morning, when you lie down at night, and when you are AT THE GROCERY STORE! (I added to the scripture just a bit.) Consider Romans 1:20: "Since the creation of the world, God's invisible qualities ... have been clearly seen in what has been MADE ... "

So what does this have to do with grocery shopping? LOOK at what has been MADE! As you walk through the produce, notice SHAPES, and COLORS. Tell you children, "God MADE this." Have them touch, and smell  and see. THANK GOD for eyes, and nose and fingers. Feel a potato, touch an onion, smell some fennel (I LOVE fennel!). What do you see that is orange? Can you find something yellow? Play the I SPY® game. Have them close their eyes and smell mint, rosemary, basil or cilantro. Thank God for your tongue ... we can taste all the good food He has made. Go to the dairy case. Ask, "Where do we get milk and eggs?" Thank God for cows and hens, and farmers! Make animal noises. Go ahead ... embarrass yourself!! Your kids will LOVE IT! (I should know. I dress in a costume and embarrass my kids all the time!)

A great adventure in parenting is looking for and finding GOD IS EVERYWHERE! Now, were all my trips to the grocery a glorious parenting experience? HA! No. I always HOPE for successful teaching moments, even the time my son knocked over a display and sent jars of spaghetti sauce crashing. What a mess. But I put on a brave face and said, "WOW! RED IS EVERYWHERE!" *Clean-up on aisle 3 …*

REMEMBER TO HAVE FUN

Sometime in my late 20s, B.C. (Before Children), I attended a beach retreat and happened to be hanging out with the speaker, who was a pastor. We were having a nice conversation when he spotted his kids and sternly yelled, "Hey, come here!" I was shocked this man would speak to his children that way … and right in front of me and others. They ran over and he grabbed each by one arm and angrily said, "Now you two listen to me! You are going to be in big trouble, BIG TROUBLE. DO YOU HEAR ME?" The two children nodded and were smiling. I was confused. "We are leaving right now and going home IF you do not have the BEST TIME OF YOUR LIFE!! Now go out there and have FUN OR ELSE!!!" They laughed and ran off to play. Whew! I was relieved, and we all laughed. What a performance! We all thought he was angry, but I realized his kids had seen it all before. I have never forgotten that moment. That guy was just plain silly. I liked him right away! He knew how to make things FUN. That is ENTHUSIASTIC ENJOYMENT!

I heard about this one: It was a hot day and a family went to get ice cream. They walked out with those yummy, sticky ice cream cones, and the 3-year old promptly dropped his on the sidewalk. He let out a wail. Daddy to the rescue! "Quick! Take off your shoes!" The crying little boy looked up, confused. "Take off your shoes and step in it!" Those tears dried up! The little guy put his bare toes in that cold stuff and began to giggle. He squished it around, howled with laughter, and made a huge mess! I'm sure the mommy was digging in her bag for some wipes, but it saved the day! Everyone had a great time watching, and it made a memory of laughter. That is JOY IN THE JOURNEY.

One day in my kitchen in Mobile, Alabama, I had a girlfriend over and we were chatting while I cleaned. My children, two and four, were around. Four year old Marilyn was playing in her room and Christopher was in the backyard swinging a stick (I think). Marilyn proudly came into the kitchen showing us her new crown, dress, and little high heeled plastic shoes. I should have taken a picture. The brother walked in just at that moment. She looked at him, twirled and said, "Look at me! I'm a Princess!" That little two-year old boy looked at her, raised his stick, and yelled, "KILL THE

PRINCESS!" She screamed, he yelled, and a chase ensued. I thought I would die laughing. I mean, really? Who taught him to say that?! Chalked it up to testosterone.

GIGGLE BREAK

A mother invited some people to dinner. At the table, she turned to the 5-year-old daughter and said, "Would you like to say the blessing?" "I don't know what to say," the girl replied. "Just say what you hear Mommy say." The daughter bowed her head and said, "Lord, why on earth did I invited all these people to dinner?"

COPY CAT

Children are imitators. They watch every move, and copy our attitude and actions. Children are mirrors of our lives. That TERRIFIES ME!

Did you ever play "Copy-Cat" ? I did — a lot! I am the oldest of four children and my father was a traveling salesman. We went on road trips often and there was no TV, no DVD player, no cell phone, no hand-held electronic ANYTHING in the car. (I am *that* old!) We played games. "I Spy" for miles, "Copy Cat" until our mama begged us for the "Quiet Game."

This and that, copy cat
Whatever I do you do it too
It's a little game where we do the same ...
Ok — here we go![41]

When I sing the "Copy Cat" song at a **MISS PATTYCAKE** concert (lyrics above), I always like to refer to the verse that is its origin, Ephesians 5:1: "Therefore be imitators of God, as beloved children."

"Imitator" is a big word for a little person, and often the best way to explain a word is to show them. "Here — imitate this, do what I do ... be a copy-cat!" Jesus did this all the time! He told stories, He used illustrations, and maybe, with the children, He played games. I like to think He did.

So come on, let's play a game! You (children) copy me, I will copy Jesus, then we will both WALK IN LOVE, which is the very next verse:

"Walk in love, just as Christ loved YOU, and gave Himself up for you, an offering and sacrifice to God ..." Ephesians 5:2

Don't we love our children? Wouldn't we give ourselves for them? OF COURSE WE WOULD. And that is how God feels about us! I like these verses better from *The Message* translation:

> **"Watch what God does, then you do it, like children who learn proper behavior from their parents. Mostly what God does is LOVE YOU. Keep company with Him and learn a life of love. Observe how Christ loved us. His love was not cautious but extravagant! He didn't love in order to get something from us but to give everything of himself to us. LOVE LIKE THAT!"**
> Ephesians 5:1-2

● ● ● ● ● ● ● ● ● ● ● ● ● ● ● ● ●

See? It's all about "Copy-Cat." How do we copy God? We look at the life of Jesus! He said, "If you have seen me, you have seen the Father." (John 14:7) READ what Jesus did — mostly He loved people. He went about doing good, helping others. I like to look at the word "therefore" to find what it is "there for." It usually refers to whatever came right before it. Ephesians 4:32 comes before the "therefore" of 5:1, so what does it say?

> **"Be kind to one another, tenderhearted, forgiving one another, just as God in Christ also has forgiven you."**

● ● ● ● ● ● ● ● ● ● ● ● ● ● ● ● ●

Let's copy THAT! If we, as parents, will ask the Father to create this lifestyle of love, kindness, forgiveness in US — then our children will SEE it, and naturally copy us as we instruct them. Together, we will COPY JESUS!

I realize, in the "hullabaloo" of life with babies, toddlers, and/or preschoolers, all this is easier said than done! In the seemingly endless diapers, bottles, sippy cups and spills, messy play area, crayons, Goldfish Crackers®, mountains of laundry, dishes, and going, going, going, take a moment — breathe — look up — THANK GOD (by faith) in all of it and REMEMBER THIS: "For it is GOD who works in us both to WILL and to DO His good pleasure." (Philippians 2:13) [*emphasis mine*]

THAT, my friend, is the key. It takes the pressure off us to "DO" it ourselves ... to get it all RIGHT! This is God's work IN us and THROUGH us. Can we love our children well? HE can love them well THROUGH US. Can we always be kind? Can we always forgive? God, the Holy Spirit is alive in us, and, as we give Him permission, He lives that beautiful LOVE LIFE through us and it spills onto our little ones. COPY THAT!

IDEAS WORTH IMITATING

🖐 **Practice Gratitude** — Give thanks in ALL things. (Colossians 3:16)

🖐 **Practice Prayer** — Call on Jesus OUT LOUD … Ask, seek, knock. (Matthew 7:7)

🖐 **Practice Serving** — Do service projects with your kids … "Faith without works is dead." (James 2:26)

🖐 **Practice Bible Memory** — Learn scripture together, sing the Word, pray scriptures back to God. "I have hidden your word in my heart …" (Psalm 119:118)

🖐 **Practice Family Worship** — MAKE TIME to thank, praise, teach, and worship the Lord as a family. (Deuteronomy 6:6-7)

NOTHING IS TOO SMALL

It was a normal busy day. My kids were little and we were going … somewhere. I buckled Christopher into the car seat, ran back in the house to grab my purse and gather "stuff," and hurry Marilyn along. I opened my purse to get the car keys. Not there. I rushed into the kitchen to look on the counter. Not there. Were they on the dresser in the bedroom?

Not there. I looked in the bathroom, the closet, and again in the living room. Now, I was really frustrated! Before I became frantic I yelled (yes, I yelled), "LORD JESUS! WHERE ARE MY KEYS?" Then I stopped, closed my eyes, and waited. It took a few seconds, but into my mind came the picture of my jacket laying over a chair in my daughter's room — right where I'd left it yesterday … with my keys in the pocket. "THANK YOU!" I grabbed those keys and we were on our way. (The Holy Spirit is brilliant!) But wait … there's more! A few days later we were headed out again and I instructed Marilyn to find her shoes. Soon I heard her 3-year old voice loudly say, "LORD JESUS! WHERE ARE MY SHOES?"

Are you convinced that God cares about your life? Of course your answer is "yes." But I mean your LIFE. The daily stuff … the everyday cleaning, shopping, cooking, working, eating, drinking, dressing, playing, walking around, gotta get it done life. Have you embraced the idea that God wants to live all of that life WITH you, and give you JOY in this journey? Just in case you have listened to the LIE that God is somehow too busy to be bothered with the little things, remember He cares so much. He knows exactly how many HAIRS are on our heads! (Luke 12:7, Matthew 10:30) With babies/toddlers/preschoolers, life is full of little stuff. It all matters to them AND to God.

PATTYCAKE DAILY IDEAS

So here's what I want you to do, God helping you: Take your everyday, ordinary life — your sleeping, eating, going-to-work, and walking-around life — and place it before God as an offering. Embracing what God does for you is the best thing you can do for him. Don't become so well-adjusted to your culture that you fit into it without even thinking. Instead, fix your attention on God. You'll be changed from the inside out. Readily recognize what He wants from you, and quickly respond to it. Unlike the culture around you, always dragging you down to its level of immaturity, God brings the best out of you, develops well-formed maturity in you." Romans 12:1-2 (*The Message*)

1. **PUT ON A PRESCHOOL FACE:** eyes open, inviting smile

Your face can communicate God's love. Make a point to be happy to see them. Try this: "I'm so glad to see your face this morning," or "YAY — you are HERE!" Let your love and attention show on your face.

My children attended a mother's day-out program once a week when they were about 2 and 3. I can't remember the woman's name who greeted us, but I can still see her smiling face and hear her voice because she always said the same thing to my children, "Hey, my loves." On paper this doesn't look the way it sounded to me, but my daughter always wanted to go. She felt loved. Thank you, precious grandmother at Cottage Hill Baptist in Mobile, Alabama for loving my children!

2. **GET ON THEIR LEVEL:** OK … you might have to get on your knees for this. The floor really is your friend. Can you get your face close to theirs? Take time to make eye contact. Go on, sit in that little chair, get down on your knees, grab a pillow if you must, pull them into your lap. The floor really is your friend.

I love when I get hand-drawn, usually crayon pictures from my little friends. Almost without fail they picture **MISS PATTYCAKE** with big feet (which is true of me), looonnnggg legs, little triangle for a dress. They try to draw the red heart but it is usually a lump. Loonngg arms with sticky outy fingers, small round head, hat, and huge red mouth (it's the lipstick). I have a collection of these fabulous pictures. This is the way they see me … I'm tall, and on stage I seem even taller. They are far from my face. But YOU can get on their level.

3. **HAVE RITUALS:** Rituals, repetition and structure help communicate a sense of security. I grew up with Mr. Rogers. I loved that he always, always sang the same greeting song, he changed from a coat to a sweater, he

changed his shoes, and he always said, "Hello, friend." His structure was comforting to me and I anticipated what came next. Try it — start with the children in your care. You can say, every day, "This is the day God has made!" Choose a theme song. By the way, they don't care if you sing well ... Mr. Rogers didn't. ☺ Here are ideas for structure: story time, prayer time, check the weather, play time, nap time, snack time, exploring (i.e., nature walk, read an I Spy© book), and game time. Little children thrive on repetition. Anticipate being reminded about leaving anything out.

4. LET THEM EXPLORE: Ask them questions. Don't tell them everything ... let them tell you. Act surprised when you hear a common sound (door bell, telephone, thunder, baby crying, dog barking, car horn, etc.). Then ask, "What was that?" Ask your children, "What is God like?" "What does God say?" You may be surprised and touched by their answers. They often give us insight we are too big to see.

Use the phrase, "I wonder ... " to help children think, respond and problem solve. For example, "I wonder what we should do about all these dirty dishes?" Children are born with an abundance of curiosity (but, I'm not telling you anything new.) They seem to constantly ask, "when, where, why, how, what?" They believe everything is possible — they don't make assumptions. They swim in the sea of possibilities. Shouldn't we all be like that? Why, yes! Jesus said,

"Truly I tell you, unless you change and become like little children, you will never enter the kingdom of heaven."
(Matthew 18:3)

6. SILENCE is good: Whisper to get their attention. Encourage them to learn how to listen for God. Have a designated quiet time and practice being still. That's not easy for most children, but you can make a game of it. Begin with little bits of time ... 30 seconds can seem like a long time to them. Ask your child to make his toes be quiet, then legs, then arms, then head, then breathe. You may find it helps both of you.

7. LISTEN: Pay attention to the details of their lives. Most children want to talk. They want to talk about ... everything. They are figuring stuff out as they talk. "I fell down yesterday, see my Band-Aid®? We went to the store, mommy got mad, Logan hit me, I don't like carrots ... " When we listen, we become a friend. And, oh my, the things you may hear. Our attention communicates LOVE.

8. MUSIC IS "MAGIC": Sing songs about everything! (Ephesians 5:20) I probably say too much about this ... but it is TRUE and it WORKS! Music is the glue that makes words stick to our brains.

What happens in your mind when you hear these words: "I am stuck on Band-Aids®, 'cause a Band-Aid®'s stuck on me!" How about … "My bologna has a first name … " Or … "Like a good neighbor, _____." Did you finish that line? Could you hear the music in your head? OF COURSE YOU COULD! And why? Because it is MUSIC — and music lives in our brain in an INDELIBLE way.

Many of my earliest memories are musical. My mother tells stories of me at age three singing "Jesus Loves Me" at the top of my lungs to anyone who would listen … at the grocery store, at the gas station, out the window to passersby. I would lie in bed at night and recount the events of the day in a spontaneous, made up song.

Later, as a mother of preschoolers, I always looked for a way to make "the job a game." AND MY METHOD WAS ALWAYS MUSIC! (Mary Poppins helped.) Have you seen all the music products available for our babies? They guarantee mathematical and scientific aptitude. They tell us to play music and see a child's vocabulary increase, prepare them for school, even teach them to read! Companies promote all kinds of music for little ones — even music for babies *in utero*. Scientific research tells us there is something "magical" about music.

Look at this research:[42]
Music speaks in a language that children instinctively understand. It draws children (as well as adults) into its orbit, inviting them to match its pitches, incorporate

its lyrics, move to its beat, and explore its emotional and harmonic dimensions in all their beauty and depth. Meanwhile, its physical vibrations, organized patterns, engaging rhythms, and subtle variations interact with the mind and body in manifold ways, naturally altering the brain in a manner that one-dimensioned rote learning cannot. Children are happy when they are bouncing, dancing, clapping, and singing with someone they trust and love. Even as music delights and entertains them, it helps mold their mental, emotional, social, and physical develop-ment — and gives them the enthusiasm and the skills they need to begin to teach themselves.

BENEFITS OF USING MUSIC WITH CHILDREN:

- Begin to communicate and connect with him even before he is born.
- Stimulate brain growth in the womb and throughout early childhood.
- Positively affect his emotional perceptions and attitudes from prebirth onward.
- Provide patterns of sound on which he can build his understanding of the physical world.
- Reduce his level of emotional stress or physical pain, even in infancy.

- Enhance his motor development, including the grace and ease with which he learns to crawl, walk, skip, and run.
- Improve his language ability, including vocabulary, expressiveness, and ease of communication.
- Introduce him to a wider world of emotional expression, creativity, and aesthetic beauty.
- Enhance his social abilities.
- Improve his reading, writing, mathematical, and other academic skills, as well as his ability to remember and to memorize.
- Introduce him to the joys of community.
- Help him create a strong sense of his own identity.

● ● ● ● ● ● ● ● ● ● ● ● ● ● ● ● ● ●

"It is amazing to think that music and rhythmic verbal sounds, which have been available to us throughout our lives, can have such a powerful effect on the mind and body. Yet the evidence is indisputable. There's far more to good music than meets the ear. Wisely used, it can create a healthy and stimulating sound world for your family and profoundly enhance your child's growth."

-Don Campbell
The Mozart Effect for Children:
Awakening Your Child's Mind,
Health and Creativity with Music

Do you remember Charlie Brown's teacher? Remember what she always said? "WA-WA-WA WAWA-WA-WA." RIGHT!? No one knows what the poor woman was talking about because she was TALKING! Now, if she had been SINGING, we would remember.

LAW OF REQUISITE VARIETY

Did you take physics in high school or college? You may remember bumping into this: disequilibrium = life. This is the law of requisite variety. The survival of any system depends on its capacity to cultivate VARIETY in its internal structures. How does this apply to parenting? Simply put … MIX IT UP!

Be aware of all three learning styles and use them with your children: Some children learn best by hearing, some by seeing and some by touching … remember to MIX IT UP since a combination of styles makes a better "glue."[43]

LET'S CELEBRATE

PEOPLE LOVE PARTIES! Celebrating is a BIG deal. It is a big deal to God. Just think about the times He commanded His people to take vacations and have big dinners together.

In the Bible, they are called feasts or festivals, and there are seven of them during one calendar year. Jesus' first miracle was at a wedding party. He made sure they had plenty of wine for celebrating! Celebrating is a good and healthy thing to do. It is especially effective in little lives. So don't wait until their birthday or Christmas, find a reason to rejoice!

- ○ Potty training
- ○ First trip to the dentist
- ○ A new baby in the family
- ○ Starting school
- ○ School is OUT
- ○ He grew an inch
- ● Learned to ride a bike
- ○ Learned to tie shoes
- ○ Caught a ball 10 times
- ○ Learned a song
- ○ Memorized a Bible verse
- ○ Memorized the books of the Bible
- ○ (They can do it! Use music!)
  Told someone about Jesus

Have you heard these words,

"Look Mommy, I DID IT ALL BY MYSELF!"

YAHOO! HAVE A PARTY.

Make cupcakes, have a spur of the moment parade. DANCE and make up a silly song (*You tied your shoes, good for you! You tied your shoes, something NEW! YAY! Good for you!*)

Draw a picture of the event. Make a "memory box" and put in a scrap of something so you will remember. Make a t-shirt, plant a tree or a flower, make a "tradition," create a PROCLAMATION (*Hear Ye, Hear Ye, May it be Known by ALL that _____ rode his bicycle all by himself today.*)

When my daughter was five, she broke her arm so we had a CAST party! Friends and family came to our house to sign her cast.

Show your children how you celebrated them before they were born. Do you have pictures of a baby shower, gifts, preparing their room, baptism, etc?

Don't forget to REWARD them for good things — obedience and achievement. God rewards our obedience both here and in eternity! (Matthew 5:12, Hebrews 11:6)

If you like to know you are doing things God's way (and I do) and you need some encouragement about a lifestyle of celebrating, check out this verse:

"Sing hymns instead of drinking songs! Sing songs from your heart to the Christ. Sing praises over everything, any excuse for a song to God the Father in the name of our Master, Jesus Christ." Ephesians 5:18-20 (*The Message*)

LAUGH A LOT
(record your giggles before you forget)

Our daughter was sitting in my husband's lap as he read a Bible story to her. She was looking at his face intently. He paused and said, "Isn't that a wonderful story? And, God loves you just like He loved Daniel and took care of him in the lion's den." Marilyn was gazing up and nodding. She said, "Daddy?" "Yes, sweetheart." "Why do you have hair in your nose?"

Garrett (age 4):
"Daddy, when I grow up I want to be a doctor!"
Proud dad: "That's great, son."
Garrett: "Or, maybe a dinosaur."

● ● ● ● ● ● ● ● ● ● ● ● ● ● ● ● ●

Reese (age 3) in church:
"Our Father, Who does art in heaven,
Harold is His Name."

• • • • • • • • • • • • • • • • • • •

Melanie (age 5)
asked her Granny how old she was.
Granny replied she was so old she didn't remember
any more. Melanie said, "If you don't remember,
you just look in the back of your panties.
Mine say five to six."

• • • • • • • • • • • • • • • • • • •

Steven (age 3)
hugged and kissed his Mom
good night. "I love you so much that when you die I'm
going to bury you outside my bedroom window."

• • • • • • • • • • • • • • • • • • •

Brittany (age 4)
had an earache and wanted a pain killer.
She tried in vain to take the lid off the bottle.
Seeing her frustration, her Mom explained
it was a childproof cap and she'd have to
open it for her. Eyes wide with wonder,
the little girl asked:
"How does it know it's me?"

• • • • • • • • • • • • • • • • • • •

Susan (age 4)

was drinking juice when she got
the hiccups. "Please don't give me this juice again,"
she said. "It makes my teeth cough."

● ● ● ● ● ● ● ● ● ● ● ● ● ● ●

Marc (age 4)

was engrossed in a young couple
that were hugging and kissing in a restaurant.
Without taking his eyes off them,
he asked his dad:
"Why is he whispering in her mouth?"

● ● ● ● ● ● ● ● ● ● ● ● ● ● ●

Clinton (age 5)

was in his bedroom looking worried.
When his Mom asked what was troubling him,
he replied, "I don't know what'll happen
with this bed when I get married.
How will my wife fit in it?"

● ● ● ● ● ● ● ● ● ● ● ● ● ● ●

James (age 4)

was listening to a Bible story.
His dad read: "The man named Lot
was warned to take his wife and flee
out of the city, but his wife looked back
and was turned to salt."
Concerned, James asked:
"What happened to the flea?"

Marcus (my nephew, age 4)
ran into the surf on his very first beach visit.
A wave crashed over him
and he came up angry and sputtering.
Which hands on his little hips he yelled,
"Mommy! Who put salt in this water?!"

Tammy (age 4)
was with her mother when they met
an elderly, rather wrinkled woman her Mom knew.
Tammy looked at her for a while and then asked,
"Why doesn't your skin fit your face?"

Alice (my niece, age 4)
asked my mother if they could sing that song
about hiking to heaven. No one was sure
which song she meant until, some time later,
it began to play on a CD and she said,
"That's it!" In the song, Be Thou My Vision,
the lyric is "High King of Heaven ... "

A little boy eyed me
after a concert in a church somewhere.
I was sitting in a chair in full
Miss PattyCake costume.

His mother approached me.
"Oh he just loves you! He watches you
all the time on TV." He hung back ...
he wasn't too sure about me.
I did my usual, "Hi there, what's your name?"
He said, "Are you a real, live, HUMAN PERSON?"

MY ALL TIME FAVORITE:

The Sunday morning prayer I think this Mom will
never forget ... "Dear Lord," the minister began,
with arms extended toward heaven and a rapturous
look on his upturned face. "We thank Thee that
Thou dost remember that we are but dust ... "
He took a breath and would have continued,
but at that moment her daughter who was
listening leaned over and asked quite audibly
in her shrill little four-year-old voice,
"Mommy, what is BUTT dust?"

IMPERATIVE

My maternal grandmother was a strict southern lady. She was famous for saying, "Dahlin', you should nevuh end youwuh sentence with a prepuhzishun and nevuh wear white aftuh Labuh Day." She was a hoot! She studied En-  glish at Columbia University in NYC, and voice at Julliard School of Music in the 1920s, and that was somethin' else for a young woman from Montgomery, Alabama. In our family, she was the "language sheriff." I come by it generationally ... my children call me a "grammar geek." I do not say everything correctly, but I fuss about it. So I am well qualified to educate you about the exclamation point.

ex·cla·ma·tion

noun \[ek-skluh-mey-shuhn]
    : a sharp or sudden cry : a word, phrase,
    or sound that expresses a strong emotion
    1. a sharp or sudden utterance
    2. vehement expression[44]

That is the name of the grammatical marker. Here is the type of directive it implies:

im·per·a·tive

adjective \[im-per-uh-tiv]
    : very important grammar : having the form
    that expresses a command rather than a
    statement or a question: expressing a
    command in a forceful and confident way[45]

The notation of an exclamtion point literally means *DO IT, NOT OPTIONAL.*

Remember, "HALLELUJAH" is always followed by an exclamation point in the Bible. Go ahead, flip open to the Psalms and see for yourself.

This (!) IMPERATIVE chapter is written to spur you into action!

Hebrews 10:24 says:
**"Let us consider how to SPUR
(stir up, stimulate and incite)
one another to love
and helpful deeds and noble activities."**

• • • • • • • • • • • • • • • • • •

It is our JOB, our privilege, our responsibility, our JOY to hear what God has to say, and DO IT! In an effort to "spur you on," let's see what the Word of God has to say about children:

• • • • • • • • • • • • • • • • • •

**"Hear, O Israel: the Lord our God is one Lord
[the only Lord]. And you shall love the Lord
your God with all your [mind and] heart and
with your entire being and with all your might.
And these words, which I am commanding
you this day shall be [first] in your [own]
minds and hearts; [then] You shall whet and
sharpen them so as to make them penetrate,
and teach and impress them diligently upon
the [minds and] hearts of your children, and
shall talk of them when you sit in your house
and when you walk by the way, and when you
lie down and when you rise up."**

Deuteronomy 6:4-7
(Amplified Bible)

• • • • • • • • • • • • • • • • • •

"Teach them to your children, talking about them when you sit at home and when you walk along the road, when you lie down and when you get up."

Deuteronomy 11:19 (NIV)

• • • • • • • • • • • • • • • • •

"Tell it to your children, and let your children tell it to their children, and their children to the next generation."

Joel 1:3

• • • • • • • • • • • • • • • • •

"The secret things belong to the Lord our God, but the things which are revealed belong to us and to our children forever … "

Deuteronomy 29:29

• • • • • • • • • • • • • • • • •

"Keep His commands, which I am giving you today, so that it may go well with you and your children after you and you may live long in the land the Lord your God gives you."

Deuteronomy 4:40

• • • • • • • • • • • • • • • • •

"Only be careful, and watch yourselves so that you do not forget the things your eyes have seen or let them slip from your heart as long as you live. Teach them to your children and to their children after them. "

Deuteronomy 4:9

● ● ● ● ● ● ● ● ● ● ● ● ● ● ● ● ● ●

"The promise (of salvation) is
for you and for your children ..."
Acts 2:39

● ● ● ● ● ● ● ● ● ● ● ● ● ● ● ● ● ●

"At that time Jesus said, 'I praise you Father,
Lord of heaven and earth, because you
have hidden these things from the wise and
learned, and revealed them to little children.'"
Matthew 11:25

● ● ● ● ● ● ● ● ● ● ● ● ● ● ● ● ● ●

"We will not hide them from the children;
we will tell the next generation the praise-
worthy deeds of the Lord ... He commanded
our forefathers to teach their children, so the
next generation would know the law, even
the children yet to be born, and they in turn
would tell their children."
Psalm 78:4-6

● ● ● ● ● ● ● ● ● ● ● ● ● ● ● ● ● ●

"He who fears the LORD has a secure
fortress and for his children it will be a refuge."
Proverbs 14:26

● ● ● ● ● ● ● ● ● ● ● ● ● ● ● ● ● ●

"All your sons will be taught by the LORD,
and great will be your children's peace."
Isaiah 54:13

● ● ● ● ● ● ● ● ● ● ● ● ● ● ● ● ● ●

**"As for me, this is my covenant with them,"
says the LORD. 'MY SPIRIT, who is on you,
and my words that I have put in your mouth
will not depart from your mouth, or from the
mouths of your children, or from the mouths
of their descendants from
this time on and forever,' says the LORD."**
Isaiah 59:21

● ● ● ● ● ● ● ● ● ● ● ● ● ● ● ● ● ●

It is no secret what God is requiring of us. He has clearly told us in Deuteronomy 6:4-8 (above), and Jesus echoed this command in Luke 10:27 and in Matthew 22:37.

Be encouraged that you are placed and privileged to parent. This is something you CAN DO. You can share God's big love with little lives. Don't quit. Never give up.

So, as you diligently work each day to tell these little ones about God, be encouraged by these words:

**"Let's not get tired of doing good, because in
time we'll have a harvest if we don't give up."**
Galatians 6:9

● ● ● ● ● ● ● ● ● ● ● ● ● ● ● ● ● ●

Therefore, my beloved brothers, be you steadfast,
unmovable, always abounding in the work
of the Lord, for as much as you know that
your labor is not in vain in the Lord."
I Corinthians 15:58

HALLELUJAH FOR THAT!

George Barna of the Barna Research Group has done much writing on families.

In *Revolutionary Parenting*, Barna notes that there are three dominant approaches to parenting currently operative in the United States:[46]

- *Parenting by default* is termed the path of least resistance. In this approach, parents do whatever comes naturally to the parent, as influenced by cultural norms and traditions. The objective is to keep everyone — parent, child, and others — as happy as possible, without having the process of parenting dominate other important or prioritized aspects of the parent's life.

- *Trial-and-error* parenting is a common alternative. This approach is based on the notion that every parent is an amateur, there are no absolute guidelines to follow, and the best parents can do is to experiment, observe outcomes, and improve based upon their successes and failures. In this incremental approach, the goals of parenting are to continually improve and to perform better than most other parents.

● *Revolutionary* parenting was the least common approach. Such nurturing requires the parent to take God's words on life and family at face value, and to apply those words faithfully and consistently.

Perhaps the most startling difference in these approaches has to do with the desired outcomes. "*Parenting by default* and *trial-and-error parenting* are both approaches that enable parents to raise their children without the effort of defining their life," Barna explained. "*Revolutionary parenting*, which is based on one's faith in God, makes parenting a life priority. Those who engage in *revolutionary parenting* define success as intentionally facilitating faith-based transformation in the lives of their children, rather than simply accepting the aging and survival of the child as a satisfactory result."[44]

Let's consider again the Stephen Covey statement, "Begin with the end in mind."[45] If you are holding a precious baby, if you are chasing a toddler, if you never sit still with a "terrific 2," if you are busy all day with a 3-year old, if you are teaching Sunday School to a preschooler, if you are a grandparent of any of these ages, then YOU have the PRIVILEGE of helping shape a life for ETERNITY! How incredible is that?!

GIGGLE BREAK

A mother was preparing pancakes for her sons, Kevin 5, and Ryan 3. The boys began to argue over who would get the first pancake. Their mother saw the opportunity for a moral lesson. "If Jesus were sitting here, He would say, 'Let my brother have the first pancake, I can wait.'" Kevin turned to his younger brother and said, "Ryan, you be Jesus!"

DO IT: TELL THE GOOD NEWS

Tell your children about God, Jesus and the Bible.

1-2-3-4-5-6-7
Jesus made a way to heaven!
Colors, Numbers, ABCs

(lyrics by Jean C. Thomason)[46]

I think that about sums it up. Sometimes the simplest answer works! The gospel is simple. Jesus did for us what we could not, cannot do for ourselves. No one ever could. No amount of trying, working, trying harder, sacrificing, slaving, giving, being good, or any other form of effort is enough. It's like my friend, Amazing Grace (cartoon book character in **MISS PATTYCAKE** videos), says:

> "Well my dears, from the very beginning God wanted each one of us to be His very own child, and live with Him forever. But because of our sin, you know, all the wrongs things we think and do, we could never be good enough no matter how hard we tried. But I'm so glad that God made a way. The Bible says in John 3:16 that God loved the world so much that He sent His only Son, Jesus, to die on the cross. And whoever believes in Him will have life everlasting! You see, nobody loves you like God, and THAT'S THE TRUTH!"

So, there it is ... simple! "Whoever believes in Him ..." (John 3:16) I am not telling you it is EASY to believe, but it is simple. Jesus told the disciples that we should "become like little children." (Matthew 18:3) Children are helpless. They need us for everything. They can't eat, dress, clean themselves, find shelter, or stay safe without help. We should see ourselves like that. We need God's help for EVERYTHING. Jesus said it well, "I am the vine, you are the branches. Apart from me, you can do (wait for it) ... NOTHING!" (John 15:5) [*emphasis mine*] THIS IS THE GOSPEL — *The Message* — the GOOD NEWS! Jesus did everything needed for us to know Him, and live with Him forever.

Tell your children the good news! I'll help make it easier with the **MISS PATTYCAKE** song, "Give Me Five He's Alive":[48]

1. Jesus was born — He came to earth on Christmas morn
2. He LOVES YOU. He lived a life so good and true
3. For you and me ... He gave his life on Calvary
4. There is so much more! 3 days later He JUMPED from the grave, then He went to heaven! And now, He prays for you and me ... EVERY DAY!
5. HE'S ALIVE — JESUS IS ALIVE!!

That right there is the GOOD STUFF! The TRUE stuff. Remember what that sign at the mall said?

A child's mind is like Jell-O®.
The idea is to put the good things in before it sets.

WRITE IT DOWN!

My daddy (aka Papa Roy) is famous in our family for these three words ...

"Write it down!"

If we wanted something from him or tried to tell him something, his response was, "Write it down." My whole life, Daddy used a Day-Timer®. Daddy (now retired) was a brilliant engineer, super organized and could develop and maintain systems that would make my head spin. As the oldest of four children, our house was in constant motion … activities, church, school, clubs … and the only way to keep track was to … write it down. To this day, I follow my father's example. Obviously, it's good advice. So check this out! God said to Moses:

> "Write these commandments that I've given you today on your hearts. Get them inside of you and then get them inside your children. Talk about them wherever you are, sitting at home or walking in the street; talk about them from the time you get up in the morning to when you fall into bed at night. Tie them on your hands and foreheads as a reminder; inscribe them on the doorposts of your homes and on you city gates."
> Deuteronomy 6:6-9
> (*The Message*)

God knows that we forget stuff. First, He told us to write it down. Then, He gave us other ways to remember. "Tie them on your hands" (like bracelets) "and foreheads" (hat, bandanna, headband), "write them on the doorposts" (a mezuzah, a wreath on the door with scripture, a plaque), "and on your city gates," (wouldn't that be amazing. It does exist in some places, like on the walls of the Supreme Court!)

Because of that biblical directive, this is what my family decided to do: Inspired by a trip to the great St. Peter's Basilica in Rome where all the words of Matthew 16:17-18 are painted in enormous letters around the entire wall just next to the ceiling, I had an artist friend paint scripture as a border in our entrance hall, our living room, and kitchen. My husband and I chose the words we wanted on our walls. For us, they were a powerful reminder of the way God wants us to daily live ... JOYFULLY!

> "Let the Word of Christ — *The Message* — have the run of the house. SING, SING YOUR HEARTS OUT TO GOD! Let every detail in your lives — words, actions, whatever — be done in the name of the Master, Jesus, thanking God the Father every step of the way." Colossians 3:16-17 (*The Message*)

A personal note: Our favorite place in downtown Franklin, Tennessee is the Irish restaurant. The fish and chips are great! In addition to the food, the thing that draws me to this warm, noisy, friendly eatery is what is written near the ceiling around the narrow, long room. It's a portion of a lengthy poem, "The Breastplate of St. Patrick" which tradition says he wrote in 433 A.D.:[51]

Christ be with me, Christ within me,
Christ behind me, Christ before me,
Christ beside me, Christ to win me,
Christ to comfort and restore me.
Christ beneath me, Christ above me,
Christ in quiet, Christ in danger,
Christ in hearts of all that love me,
Christ in mouth of friend and stranger.

IS IT WORTH IT?

We dare not neglect our role in spiritual formation. It is the best gift we can give the children in our care.

Once again a word from our friend, George Barna: "The most significant aspect of every person's life is his or her spiritual health."

Did you know I'm related to a writer? You probably haven't heard of her, but she has written countless Bible studies, letters, notes, permissions, menus, real estate contracts, and poems by the hundreds. This fabulous woman has influenced my life from my earliest days. Can you guess who she is? That right! My mother ... Bebe Herren Costner. I found this gem among her writings:

When my daughters, Jean and Lynn, were 5 and 6, a movie called 'The Bible' came out. It began with the creation and went through Abraham and Isaac. Taking the girls was a treat, going to the big theater for their first time. Little did I know how frightening the last scene would be!

Abraham takes his only son up the mountain, ties him to an altar, and proceeds to raise the large, ugly knife over him. I heard Lynn gasp, making that sob sound just before the tears, and I quickly reached over Jean to calm her. Too late. I saw that Jean had already turned to her little sister and I heard her insistent voice as she loudly whispered, 'It's OK, he won't kill him. I read the book.'

What a moment! Not only was Lynn instantly soothed, but I was also given the deep reward all parents desire: Jean 'got it'!! All that time poured into the bedtime reading was worth it. I knew she could use what she had heard from the Bible in a real life situation and use it to be helpful. It is a privilege to pass this on to encourage all you young mothers who struggle with the daily chores. It's worth it. Just read The Book.

So now you understand how I knew to tell my children early about God. My mother set a good example. At this writing, my own children are 22 and 23 years old. I still talk to them about God … all the time. (They are pretty sick of those **MISS PATTYCAKE** songs.) I agree with my mother … it IS worth it.

YOU CAN DO THIS!

You have everything you need. YOU are God's perfect choice … So let's recap:

You have been **PLACED AND PRIVILEGED TO PARENT**

You have a **RARE WINDOW OF OPPORTUNITY**

You have **ACCESS TO GOD'S "ALL"**

You hold the master key … **PRAYER**

You know to begin in **INFANCY**

You have learned **SEVEN WAYS TO PRACTICE PRAISE**

You can do this with **ENTHUSIASTIC ENJOYMENT**

AND now you know it is **IMPERATIVE!**

As a fellow traveler and sister to you, I BLESS YOU in the beautiful name of the Lord Jesus. I come alongside to help hold up your arms like Aaron did for his brother Moses. And I speak to you these strong and living words:

May the Lord
bless you and protect you
May the Lord
smile on you
and be gracious to you
May the Lord show you
his favor and
give you his peace.
Amen

Numbers 6:24-27
(New Living Translation)

RESOURCES

1 Nancy Gordon and Chris Springer. *Pattycake Praise.* Integrity's Hosanna! Music. Copyright 1995 Integrity's Hosanna! Music (ASCAP) (adm. at CapitolCMGPublishing. com) All rights reserved. Used by permission.

2 Dr Caroline Leaf. drleaf.com/blog. *You are What You Think: 75-98% of Mental and Physical Illnesses Come from our Thought Life!* Dr. Caroline Leaf, Nov. 30, 2011.

3 Mahan, Melinda. *Soul Retreat for Moms.* Inspirio™/ Zondervan. 2002.

4 Meyer, FB. *The Secret of Guidance.* Chicago, IL. Moody Publishers. 2010.

5 Clare Herbert Woolston. *Jesus Loves the Little Children.* Copyright: Public Domain.

6 Whitehead, David. *Making Sense of the Bible: Rediscovering the Power of Scripture Today.* HarperOne. March 18, 2014.

7 Darlene Schacht. *Teach Them Who God Is.* www.timewarpwife.com. February 18, 2013.

8 Barna, George. *Transforming Children Into Spiritual Champions.* Regal House Publishing. Nov. 21, 2003.

[9]Ibid.

[10]Urban Child Institute. *Baby's Brain Begins Now: Conception to Age 3*. www.urbanchildinstitute.org. April 18 2011.

[11]National Center for Infants, *Toddlers and Families. Brain Development*. www.zerotothree.org.

[12]Reisser, Paul. *Complete Guide to Baby & Child Care*. Tyndale House. September 19, 1997.

[13]Barna, George. *Transforming Children Into Spiritual Champions*. Regal House Publishing. Nov. 21, 2003.

[14]Lee, R.S. *Your Growing Children and Religion*. Penguin Books, 1967 (Reprint).

[15]St. Ignatius of Loyola, Founder, Society of Jesuits. 1539. https://en.wikipedia.org/wiki/Ignatius_of_Loyola.

[16]Barna, George. *Transforming Children Into Spiritual Champions*. Regal House Publishing. Nov. 21, 2003.

[17]Forest E. Witcraft, Scholar/Teacher. "A hundred years from now ..." http://www.values.com/inspirational-quotes/4244-a-hundred-years-from-now-it-. Jan. 23, 2014.

[18]Stone, Dave. *Raising Your Kids to Love the Lord*. Thomas Nelson. Feb. 4, 2013.

[19] *Webster Dictionary*. http://www.freedictionarydefinitions.com. 2015.

[20] Katherine Lee. *Surprising Reasons Why We Need to Discipline Children*. http://childparenting.about.com.

[21] Young, Helen. Children Won't Wait: Sharing the Precious Moments of Your Baby's Childhood. Brownlow Publishing Co., Sept. 1995.

[22] Lucado, Max. *Before Amen*. Thomas Nelson. Sept. 30, 2013.

[23] Covey, Stephen R. *The Seven Habits of Highly Effective People*. Free Press. Nov. 9, 2004 (Revised Edition).

[24] Morgan, Elisa, and Kuykendall, Carol. *What Every Mom Needs*. Zondervan, May 26, 2009.

[25] Ibid.

[26] Plato. "You know that the beginning ...." *Republic*. 380 BC. https://en.wikipedia.org/wiki/Republic_(Plato).

[27] Jeanne Hendricks. Speech. MOPS International Leadership Convention. 1994.

[28] Patti Chadwick. *Lois and Eunice*. www.historyswomen.com. PC Publications, 22 Williams St., Batavia, NY 14020. www.pcpublications.org.

[29]Covey, Stephen R. *The Seven Habits of Highly Effective People*. Free Press. Nov. 9, 2004 (Revised Edition).

[30]Dr Billy Graham. http://billygrahamlibrary.org/from-billy-graham-to-the-graduate/. Excerpt from commencement address at Liberty University, Lynchburg, Va.

[31]Dr. Bruce Leafblad. Lecture. Southwest Baptist Theological Seminary.

[32]Easton, M.G. *Illustrated Bible Dictionary*. Cosimo Classics. April 15, 2005.

[33]Kendrick, Graham (Editor). *The Source: v. 2: The Worship Collection*. Kevin Mayhew Ltd. July 2001.

[34]Carruthers, William. *Westminster Shorter Catechism of the Westminster Assembly of Divines*. November 25, 1647 (1st Edition)

[35]Marshall, Catherine. *Something More*. Chosen Books, March 2002.

[36]Taylor, Jack R. *Hallelujah Factor*. Kingdom Publishing. Sept. 1999 (Revised Edition).

[37]Belden C. Lane. *Ravished by Beauty: The Surprising Legacy of Reformed Spirituality*. Oxford University Press. April 21, 2011.

[38]Pascal, Blaise. *Pensées*. Benediction Classics. April 2011.

[39]Robert B. Sherman and Richard M. Sherman. "A Spoonful of Sugar." Walt Disney Records. Copyright: 1964. https://en.wikipedia.org/wiki/A_Spoonful_of_Sugar.

[40]Steve Merkel and Jean Thomason. *Colors, Numbers, ABCs*. Integrity's Hosanna! Music(ASCAP) (adm. at CapitolCMGPublishing.com) Copyright 2002. All rights reserved. Used by permission.

[41]Nancy Gordon and Rhonda Scelsi. *Copy Cat*. Integrity's Hosanna! Music. Copyright 1995 Integrity's Hosanna! Music (ASCAP) (adm. at CapitolCMGPublishing.com) All rights reserved. Used by permission.

[42]Don Campbell. T*he Mozart Effect for Children: Awakening Your Child's Mind, Health and Creativity with Music*. Wiliam Morow / HarperColins. 2000.

[43]Call, Nicola. *The Thinking Child: Brain-Based Learning for the Early Years Foundation Stage*. Bloomsbury Academic. June 10, 2010 (2nd Edition)

[44]*Webster Dictionary*. http://www.freedictionarydefinitions.com. 2015.

[45]Ibid.

[46]Barna, George. *Revolutionary Parenting: What the Research Shows Really Works*. Tyndale Momentum. Sept. 1, 2010.

[47]Ibid.

[48]Covey, Stephen R. *The Seven Habits of Highly Effective People*. Free Press. Nov. 9, 2004 (Revised Edition).

[49]Steve Merkel and Jean Thomason. *Colors, Numbers, ABCs.* Integrity's Hosanna! Music(ASCAP) (adm. at CapitolCMGPublishing.com) Copyright 2002. All rights reserved. Used by permission.

[50]Nancy Gordon, Steve Merkel and Jean Thomason. *Give Me Five, He's Alive*. Integrity's Hosanna! MusicASCAP and Mother's Heart Music (administered by Integrity's Hosanna! Music)ASCAP. Copyright: 2002.

[51]James O'Shea. *St. Patrick's Breastplate, the poem of Ireland's greatest Saint*. http://www.irishcentral.com/roots. March 8, 2016.

[52]Barna, George. *Transforming Children Into Spiritual Champions*. Regal House Publishing. Nov. 21, 2003.

ACKNOWLEDGEMENTS

THANKS BE TO GOD! Little is much in Your upside-down Kingdom, and You chose little me for this BIG work. Astonishing! Thank You for giving me a "garment of praise" — my life is JOYFUL!

Chris Thomason for saying YES to the Miss PattyCake idea 22 years ago, and for continuing to be my partner in every way. You have labored countless hours, designing products, marketing, working backstage, selling merch, running sound, booking travel, working on schedules, babysitting, encouraging me to keep going, videoing all our children's events when I was on the road, and never minding your title, "Mr. PattyCake". Our life together is colorful! I love you.

Nancy Gordon for cleverly crafting songs which led to the brilliant idea of creating a costumed character. Thank you for bringing your idea to ME! Thank you for "spurring me on to love and good deeds". Your work is still working – YAY GOD!

Karl Horstmann for seeing and sharing our vision, creating Miss PattyCake's world, and making her a "movie star"! You love children and love using your art form to reach little ones for God's kingdom. You will see your investment in eternity!

Marilyn and Christopher for making me a MOTHER. Not that you had a choice. You have made my life full — I love you BIG MUCH.

Mama — my lifelong cheerleader – my ambassador. I have copied YOU in parenting and loving little ones. You are the original "Miss PattyCake". I'm forever grateful God put me in your family. "My boundary lines have fallen in pleasant places, indeed my heritage is beautiful to me." Psalm 16:6

Lynn and Sissy — my sisters. What would my life look like without you? I don't want to know! You have been Aaron and Hur in this project and I have finished stronger because of you. We still have "miles to go before we sleep"!

Deb Hash — my collaborator, editor, road manager, prayer warrior, stay-up-all-night-to-get-it-right FRIEND. You are faithful and true.

Sheryl Chernault for thousands of road miles, years of encouragement and all the times you said, "Write the book!" You are FABULOUS!

Kai Vilhelmsen — "Mr. Stan the Handyman" … singer, writer, actor, brother from another mother. You are AMAZERIFIC! You are valuable to the Kingdom.

Dr. Mark Wyatt for saying YES that day I "accidentally" bumped into you in a bookstore in Mobile, AL. Thanks for taking on this project and telling me I am an author! God works in jots and tittles, widows and orphans.

All @kidmin brothers and sisters who love and serve little ones - You have welcomed me into your churches, ministries, festivals, conferences, camps, parades, carnivals, parties, holiday celebrations, hospitals, homes and hearts. I have grown and learned from all of you. I am grateful.

Dr. Mark Wyatt for saying YES that day I "accidentally" bumped into you in a bookstore in Mobile, AL. Thanks for taking on this project and telling me I am an author! God works in jots and tittles, widows and orphans.

All @kidmin brothers and sisters who love and serve little ones — You have welcomed me into your churches, ministries, festivals, conferences, camps, parades, carnivals, parties, holiday celebrations, hospitals, homes and hearts. I have grown and learned from all of you. I am grateful.

Joyfully,

Jean Thomason
March 2016

CPSIA information can be obtained
at www.ICGtesting.com
Printed in the USA
LVOW02s0446240316
480468LV00007B/17/P